CREATING A SMARTER CAMPUS

APPLYING GIS

CREATING A SMARTER CAMPUS

GIS FOR EDUCATION

Edited by
Joseph Kerski
Matt Artz

Esri Press
REDLANDS | CALIFORNIA

Esri Press, 380 New York Street, Redlands, California 92373-8100

Printed in the United States of America.

ISBN: 9781589487376
Library of Congress Control Number: 2022941975

For purchasing and distribution options (both domestic and international), please visit esripress.esri.com.

On the cover: Photograph by Jacob Lund.

CONTENTS

Introduction ix
How to use this book xiii

PART 1: EDUCATORS 1

GIS project helps with food insecurity and waste 3
Palomar College

Mapping for equity and environmental justice 8
Equity Research Institute, University of Southern California

Building a geospatial legacy 12
Swiss Federal Institute of Technology

Students map ingenious route to clean water 18
Saaf water

Students see opportunities for community growth 23
Penn State University

Making GIS a statewide initiative 28
West Virginia Department of Education

High school helps students expand their analytic capabilities 31
Loudoun Valley High School

PART 2: RESEARCHERS 39

Serious game play 41
Rochester Institute of Technology

Communities see how land-use changes may affect local water quality 49
Tipping Point Planner Program

Evaluating tobacco use on a tobacco-free campus 56
University of South Carolina

Geospatial brainpower: Research on spatial reasoning 60
The Geospatial Semester at James Madison University

GIS and ancient trees reveal past temperatures and climate change 67
University of Arizona's Laboratory of Tree-Ring Research and Western Washington University

Mapping pikas' habitat to help save them 73
Nevada Department of Wildlife; University of Nevada, Reno; and San José State University

PART 3: IT SUPPORT 79

University inspires campus-wide GIS use 81
Clemson Center for Geospatial Technologies

University makes GIS accessible across campus 89
University of California San Diego

Mapping without boundaries: GIS reaches across university and beyond 93
Colorado State University

Scaling up GIS across campus 99
University of Michigan

University empowers campus-wide GIS 102
HAS University of Applied Sciences

PART 4: ADMINISTRATORS 107

School district integrates CAD and GIS for planning 109
Albuquerque Public Schools

Online schooling prompts municipalities to map digital inequities 114
Philadelphia and Palm Beach School Districts

University uses GIS to rethink campus litter management 120
Michigan State University

New university campus incorporates GIS from the outset 128
Sabah Al-Salem University City—Kuwait University

GIS improves estate management 133
University of Cambridge

It's in the wastewater: Sensing and mapping COVID-19 137
University of California San Diego

Crowdsourcing a university's facilities mapping 142
Washington State University

NEXT STEPS 148

Contributors *155*

INTRODUCTION

WE HUMANS HAVE ALWAYS BEEN FASCINATED WITH investigating our home—the earth. To understand our planet, ancient scholars in Rome, Greece, and China founded the study of geography more than 2,500 years ago. Today, geography is more relevant than ever as we grapple with issues such as climate change, economic globalization, urban sprawl, loss of biodiversity, sustainable agriculture, water quality and quantity, energy needs, cultural diversity, mass tourism, political instability, and natural hazards. As these challenges grow on a global scale, they also increasingly affect our everyday lives. To address these issues requires a populace that has a firm foundation in geography, that can see the "big picture" but also understands how patterns and trends are related, from the global to the local. Geography is concerned with all the relevant issues of our time because all these issues have a geographic component.

Geographic information system (GIS) technology offers a powerful decision-making toolbox that can be used in educational administration, educational policy, and classroom instruction. GIS offers administrators a way to visualize and manage tasks such as monitoring campus safety, mapping campus buildings and infrastructure, routing school buses, planning where and when to close schools and open new ones, and strategizing recruitment efforts. For educational policy makers, GIS provides tools to see patterns in educational achievement and decide where to target new programs.

In instruction, applying GIS helps students understand content in a variety of disciplines, not only in geography but in history, mathematics, language arts, environmental studies, chemistry, biology, and civics, among others. GIS is an inquiry-driven, problem-solving, standards-based set of tasks that incorporates field research and provides career pathways that are increasingly in demand. Geotechnologies, along with biotechnologies and nanotechnologies, are the three key skills and job markets identified by the US Department of Labor for the twenty-first century.

GIS helps students think critically and use real data while connecting them to their own community. It does so in informal, primary, secondary, and university settings and appeals to today's visual learners. Every day, on the web, in textbooks, on social media, videos, and TV, students learn about their world. They experience their community through different forms of transportation; they collect data by way of sidewalk and streamside, access videos from the internet, and gather information from sources far and wide. Managing this great wealth of data calls for using GIS.

A GIS manages location-based information and provides the tools to display and integrate it, whether it is population characteristics, economic development opportunities, or vegetation types. A GIS consists of more than just computer software; it gives users the power to link data to maps to create dynamic displays. It provides tools to visualize, query, and analyze data in ways that are not possible with traditional spreadsheets or static maps.

You do not need to teach geography to use GIS in a classroom. History teachers can watch a region change over time. Science teachers can enhance local projects with interactive maps. Numbers come alive when they represent a real place and can be visualized in a GIS. Language arts teachers can explore the richness of communication with multimedia maps. And all classes become vocational in nature when students develop skills sought by the workplace.

In their schoolwork, students can use GIS to bring value to the community. Everyone benefits when students catalog community resources, such as community gardens, open space, trails, or recycling centers; help businesses market their products; or define alternative land uses such as urban greenways. Working with businesses, agencies, or researchers, students can use GIS to display the complex fabric that is our community and our world. GIS is a tool for studying the world and all that was, is, or could be in it, at a local, regional, or global level.

Educators

Educators help students gain problem-solving and communication skills by including GIS in their instruction. Integrating information across disciplines through location reveals relationships between places and phenomena, which promotes understanding of the world around them. Today's mapping software allows sharing and inspires action.

Researchers

GIS provides data integration, analysis, visualization, and storytelling capabilities that are uniquely engineered for data with a spatial component. Designed for interoperability, GIS connects to other research tools to support open source science.

IT support

GIS has migrated to a cloud-based platform, which opens the use of GIS to a wider variety of students, faculty, and administrators, across a school, college, or university, and in the workplace beyond academia. But it also requires people who are knowledgeable in setting up and maintaining systems, including installing software, adding and managing users with varying roles, hosting data, ensuring the systems are secure, coding and configuring these systems, and performing a variety of other IT tasks.

Administrators

With timely, accurate information and spatial situational awareness, administrators can optimize the use of space; map all their water, electric, and fiber optic infrastructure; keep their campuses safe; communicate with stakeholders; and save energy. In these ways, GIS software helps institutions build and maintain engaging learning environments.

Stories and strategies

Creating a Smarter Campus: GIS for Education presents a collection of real-life stories that illustrate how education organizations use GIS to solve challenges and create better outcomes. These stories aim to help you understand how to use GIS to apply The Geographic Approach—a way to use geography to help solve problems and make better decisions—and integrate spatial reasoning into teaching, research, and management. The book concludes with a section about getting started with GIS, which provides ideas, strategies, tools, and suggested actions that organizations can adopt to build location intelligence into decision-making and operational workflows. Overall, the book presents location intelligence as another crucial layer of knowledge that managers and practitioners can add to their existing experience and expertise, offering a unique geographic perspective that can be incorporated into daily operations and planning.

If The Geographic Approach isn't currently part of an organization's decision-making processes or daily operational activities or if it isn't used to improve student outcomes, managers can use this book to start developing skills in these areas. Developing these skills does not require deep GIS expertise, nor does it require professionals to disregard all their existing experience and knowledge. The value of The Geographic Approach is that it adds another way to think about problem-solving in a real-world context.

HOW TO USE THIS BOOK

THIS BOOK IS DESIGNED TO HELP YOU FOCUS ON ISSUES that matter to you right now. It is a guide to taking the first steps with GIS and applying location intelligence to decisions and operational processes to solve common problems and create a more collaborative environment in your organization. You can use this book to identify where maps, spatial analysis, and GIS apps might be helpful in your work and then, as next steps, learn more about these resources. Learn about additional GIS resources for education by visiting the web page for this book:

go.esri.com/casc-resources

PART 1

EDUCATORS

GIS TECHNOLOGY IS CENTRAL TO DEVELOPING THRIVING communities and solving the world's most pressing environmental and social problems. Using GIS, students and scholars collect spatial data, investigate trends, predict change, compare scenarios, and propose solutions. This work doesn't simply result in additional knowledge and skills: it often leads to action by students and faculty, and even by the wider community, that leads to greater opportunity, health, resiliency, and sustainability. In this way, leading colleges and universities prepare students for meaningful careers and advance our understanding of people, places, and processes, from the local to the global scale.

In geography and geographic information science

GIS provides modern, industry-standard tools and methods for your classroom exercises and projects, whether in geography or geographic information science (GIScience). Students use the same industrial-strength GIS software used by the institutions looking to hire them after graduation. Whether you're teaching GIS fundamentals or advanced concepts, from map design and spatial analysis to machine learning and data collection using remotely piloted aerial vehicles, such as drones, a wide array of resources and GIS lessons are available to help you succeed as an educator.

Across the curriculum

You can find such resources even if you are using GIS as an instructional tool to teach another subject, such as earth or environmental science, history, mathematics, data science, engineering, or urban planning. Maps and location analytics enhance scholarship in dozens of fields by revealing patterns and relationships. These insights improve understanding and decision-making in both natural and human systems. GIS provides an integrated system for data collection, analysis, and publication that's also open and extensible. Enable access throughout your institution with enterprise licensing backed up by support and training and best practices shared by your peers.

GIS in action

This section looks at real-life stories about how students and faculty use GIS to make a positive difference on their campuses and beyond. These include addressing the serious problem of food waste, investigating areas where environmental justice is most needed, building a geospatial legacy in research and development, designing a tool to help people know whether water is safe to drink, revitalizing an urban center, incorporating GIS in K–12 education, and fostering geographic literacy with exceptional learners. These stories show that spatial thinking is being nurtured through the application of GIS on campuses across the world, from primary schools to university students, and across many disciplines.

GIS PROJECT HELPS WITH FOOD INSECURITY AND WASTE

Palomar College

ACCORDING TO THE UNITED STATES DEPARTMENT OF Agriculture (USDA), Americans throw away 30 to 40 percent of the entire US food supply.

At the same time all this food is wasted, according to research conducted by the USDA and released in 2018, 11.8 percent of Americans struggle with hunger daily and one in six children live in food-insecure households. These numbers represent conditions before the massive unemployment caused by the COVID-19 pandemic, which exacerbated the problem.

A geography professor at a Southern California college developed a community-based service-learning project that originally focused on addressing food insecurity. However, the project has expanded and now supports strategies for addressing other equity and social justice issues, implementing state restrictions on solid waste disposal, and mitigating climate change.

In 2014, Wing Cheung, a professor of geography and environmental studies at Palomar College in San Marcos, California, met with Craig Jones and Geertje Grootenhuis, representatives of local nonprofit organizations, to discuss how GIS could help address food insecurity and other equity and social justice issues through the community-based service-learning projects that Cheung envisioned for his students. Initially, he discussed using GIS to help minimize food waste.

Jones was instrumental in founding the Alliance for Regional Solutions, which coordinates and advocates for communities in the North County region of San Diego County, and the North County Food Policy Council (NCFPC), a member of the Alliance for

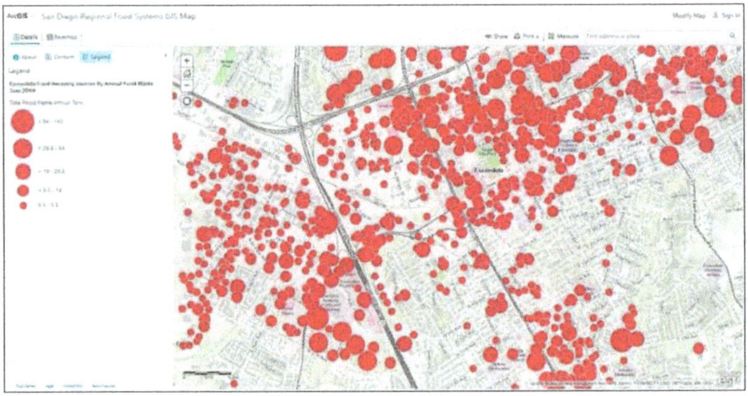

Total food waste from 2019 in tons in San Diego County, mapped by location.

Regional Solutions that assesses and supports the creation of programs to ensure that residents of North County have adequate food. Grootenhuis is the manager of the Wasted Food Prevention Program at the San Diego Food System Alliance (SDFSA), a network of more than 100 organizations working to make the current food system more equitable, healthy, and sustainable.

"After speaking with Professor Cheung, we realized that GIS could be a very useful tool for the NCFPC," said Jones. "It would allow us to better understand the nature and extent of food insecurity and the resources to address it—both existing and needed."

The State of California had recently enacted laws requiring that cities and counties reduce solid waste and reduce or recover food now in the waste stream. Communities are also required to reduce greenhouse gas emissions, which decaying food creates, because of their adverse effect on climate. To ascertain the amount of food wasted locally, the SDFSA established contact with cities in the region to obtain weekly solid waste data for local businesses.

This data is then used to calculate the tons of food waste

generated by local businesses on an annual basis. Ultimately, the datasets are provided to GIS students at Palomar College to geocode and analyze. This data is visualized as point data that is categorized based on state land-use codes and the quantity of wasted food generated at that location.

"Having this information in GIS helps our local cities address the state's mandate to plan and reduce or redirect food waste. So far, approximately half of the municipalities in San Diego County have their datasets on our GIS platform, and we continue to engage in discussions with other local cities on how they may take advantage of the platform themselves," said Jones.

"The Wasted Food Prevention Program provides technical assistance, consumer education, and network development to raise awareness about the issues of food waste," said Grootenhuis. "Our alliance between SDFSA, NCFPC, and Palomar College has opened up the powerful analytical capabilities of GIS to us. With its custom mapping tools, the technology also allows us to clearly depict the local issues that contribute to food waste, which helps prevent good food from ending up in the landfill."

The project was fully implemented in the fall semester of 2015. Cheung's students in his introductory GIS class began by geocoding the spreadsheets created by NCFPC that detailed its partners' locations. Semester by semester, both beginning and advanced GIS students at Palomar added data layers and updated existing ones. For example, students mapped the participation rate in free and reduced-price lunch programs in San Diego County schools.

Over the years, Palomar College students have used ArcMap™, ArcGIS® Pro, and ArcGIS Online to process, analyze, and share the data they received from community partners. The data is provided by a variety of sources, including local government agencies, school districts, and other community agencies in the region.

Although the project started with data layers that covered only North County, over time the value of this information has attracted the attention of local governments and nonprofits from all over San Diego County, so relevant data layers that include the entire county have been created and added.

This is particularly important because the SDFSA has substantial regional connections and the resources to market the value and use of the map throughout the region. The web map has received thousands of views and has nearly 50 layers, which can be turned on and off as needed.

Since its beginning, the partnership between NCFPC, Palomar College, and SDFSA has evolved in response to the needs of communities in the region. These service-learning projects demonstrate how GIS can enable educators to build partnerships with community organizations to address many more real-world problems. The program began by mapping existing food assistance programs and sociodemographic data to serve those in the region who suffer from food insecurity. Today, it has expanded to explore opportunities to address issues such as food waste, climate change, and transportation challenges while continuing its focus on food insecurity.

"We have found that using GIS provides us with insight into social services and equity issues far beyond the issue of food insecurity," said Jones.

The Alliance for Regional Solutions is now pursuing a grant from the State of California for planning transportation systems for disadvantaged populations living in San Diego's North County. Maps that Palomar College students have made showing the location of disadvantaged communities in relation to their current public transit options will provide the justification for the grant.

To facilitate the application process, Cheung and his students provided Jones with a data layer of census tracts in ArcGIS Online,

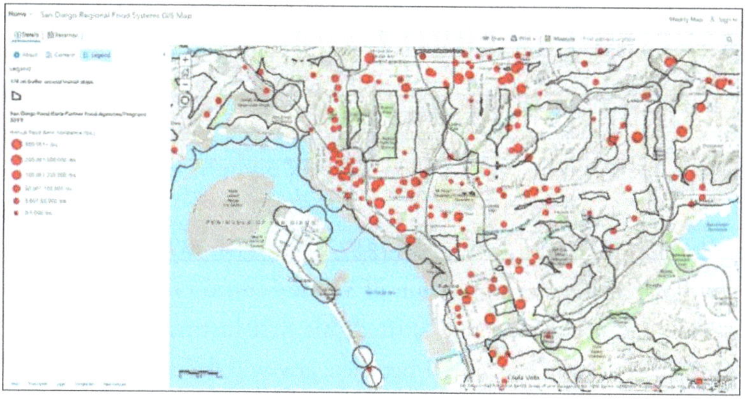

This map shows the locations of San Diego Food Bank partners, their proximity to transit stops, and the amount of food assistance they provide annually.

which enabled Jones to create custom maps that highlight the transportation needs specified in the grant proposal.

"Those involved in social justice issues in San Diego County are learning that GIS tools can be used to analyze and visualize pressing regional problems," said Cheung. "The projects developed by our partnerships with local agencies require students to apply their classroom knowledge of GIS to research, analyze, and solve real-world problems related to food insecurity and food waste in San Diego County. The program also enhances the students' communication skills, as well as their awareness of social justice and equity issues in the community."

A version of this story by Jim Baumann originally appeared in the Fall 2020 issue of *ArcUser*.

MAPPING FOR EQUITY AND ENVIRONMENTAL JUSTICE

Equity Research Institute, University of Southern California

WHEN MANUEL PASTOR FIRST SAW THE MAP SHOWING how clearly the population of South Central Los Angeles (LA) in Southern California had shifted, his first instinct was to show someone, because, he said, "I bet their jaw will drop." In just a few decades, the area's majority Black population had become an overwhelmingly majority Latino population.

The map image—one that's tailor-made for a generation accustomed to GIFs—shows those stark changes over time in a quick animation and acts like a visual thesis for Pastor's latest book, *South Central Dreams*. It's also a keen example of the power of maps in his research.

"When you show people a map, the story is so much stronger, the communications piece is so much better," Pastor said. The result can leave a viewer stunned. "That's the punch you want with the story."

The University of Southern California (USC) sociology professor and director of USC's Equity Research Institute has spent his academic career working with community activists and diving into numbers, spreadsheets, and data tables to expose inequities and promote environmental justice. He and his team of researchers also use GIS to visualize and analyze demographic and economic shifts and create the maps that share those findings.

Pastor's work with colleagues developing an Environmental Justice Screening Method is now part of California's CalEnviroScreen process, a mapping tool that helps the California Environmental Protection Agency identify communities most impacted by multiple environmental, social, and health hazards.

The Environmental Justice Screening Method has also been used by officials for Los Angeles County to help identify Green Zone neighborhoods—those in need of environmental remediation and investment.

Still seeking equity after all these years

Despite decades of palpable political awareness of environmental justice issues, solutions have only recently been incorporated into bureaucratic processes in California, Pastor said. Community activists, who were accustomed to wrangling their way into agency meetings to discuss environmental justice actions, are now often invited to participate at the onset. According to Pastor, there's been a realization that the earlier people are involved in solutions, the more amenable they'll be to the result. There's a sense of ownership.

Pastor has also recognized how important it is for social organizers to communicate closely with data managers within organizations and governments. The connection serves to effect change and foster what he calls "nerd to nerd" relationships.

After he coauthored a landmark 2007 study, "Still Toxic After All These Years," Pastor said researchers with the Bay Area Air Quality Management District backed up his research to naysayers, confirming the conclusions.

In that study, he helped show that, even controlling for wealth and land use, race played a larger role for a Bay Area resident living near environmental hazards. The report found that a Black family earning more than $100,000 was more likely to be living near a toxic waste facility than a white family earning $25,000.

In his latest book, Pastor and his coauthors looked deeply at South Central LA's population shifts.

"It's maps, it's data, and it's a qualitative story," he said of the book. "It does something else, too. It goes beneath the flash and fury to the daily lives," he said, referring to what has happened since the early 1990s. At that time, the area was an epicenter of violent divisions and had become synonymous with crime and blight. Although plenty of progress has been made since, Pastor said, stories about Black and Hispanic neighbors getting along in the community and forging common interests and collective organizations are not seen as newsworthy as the preceding conflict.

Building knowledge communities

Pastor grew up in La Puente, California, in a neighborhood bereft of greenery, near toxic hazards. It took trudging across hot asphalt to get anywhere and searching two towns over to find a public swimming pool.

While that kind of life experience can affect people in different ways, it often has a psychological impact, Pastor said. "It's insulting to be in a place where no one is planting trees. Where there are no parks. It is every part of the built landscape that is screaming at you that you are less than."

The more we can create buffers between homes and nearby industry with natural features, he said, the more positive health outcomes there will be—including self-esteem and community esteem.

In *Equity, Growth, and Community: What the Nation Can Learn from America's Metro Areas*, Pastor and his coauthor, Chris Benner, point to evidence that communities reliant on robust data sharing were better off. In their analysis, such locales were more equitable, and as a result, had more sustainable growth. In these "knowledge communities," he said, people were on the same page.

"Our ability to grow together may be fundamentally rooted in our ability to know together," he and Benner wrote in their book. Knowing where people are located has been instrumental to Pastor's work with social advocacy.

In the 2012 and 2016 presidential elections, he recognized the potential power of maps on voting outreach. By using an underlying answer in the census to estimate where recently naturalized citizens may be living, he helped give get-out-the-vote groups a guide to reaching immigrants.

They were simple maps but are still among Pastor's favorites. "Any map that changes the world to be a better place is a good map," he said.

Reasons for optimism

Despite his upbringing among environmental hazards and his long pursuit of equity, Pastor remains optimistic that better days lie ahead.

There's a streak of beating the odds in his life. For one, the university professor is the child of an undocumented immigrant with a sixth-grade education and a mother who reached 10th grade before leaving school.

He's also lived through three decades of difficult social movements. Many of those pursuits, including workers' rights, commitments to climate change intervention, community improvements, and shifting political representation, ultimately came to some fruition.

There remains dramatic inequality in our society, Pastor said, but "there's a willingness to deal with it."

A version of this story by Steve Gay originally appeared as "For Equity and Environmental Justice, USC's Manuel Pastor Knows Maps' Power" on the Esri Blog on September 23, 2021.

BUILDING A GEOSPATIAL LEGACY

Swiss Federal Institute of Technology

THE SWISS FEDERAL INSTITUTE OF TECHNOLOGY—LOCATED in Zurich, Switzerland, and better known by its Swiss name, ETH Zürich (ETHZ)—is a public research university founded by the Swiss federal government in 1854 with the mission to educate engineers and scientists. The school focuses exclusively on science, technology, engineering, and mathematics (STEM) education. ETHZ is home to 22,000 students and 540 professors from more than 120 countries and consistently ranks as a top world university.

ETHZ has ties to 21 Nobel Prize winners, including Albert Einstein and Wolfgang Pauli. The university was also home to the renowned cartographer Eduard Imhof, who is considered one of the founders of modern academic cartography. Imhof was appointed the first Swiss professor of cartography and founded the Cartographic Institute in Zurich, now the world's oldest cartography institute. Renamed in 2011, the Institute of Cartography and Geoinformation focuses on cutting-edge research related to mapping, GIS technology, spatial analytics, and more.

Between the institute and the core geoinformation-related course offerings, ETHZ has been a user of Esri products for more than 20 years and has produced several award-winning graduates. ETHZ's combination of GIS technology, advanced coursework, and geospatial research continues to support the university's ongoing mission and scientific legacy.

A legacy of geospatial technology success in the classroom

GIS software has been vital for students studying in the university's geoinformation-related programs, including geomatic engineering and planning, geospatial engineering, geomatics, and earth or environmental sciences.

Monika Niederhuber, a technical assistant and lecturer for the ETHZ environmental systems science department, structures her courses to foster a deep understanding of GIS technology and its applications. Students in these introductory-level courses learn the theoretical basics and fundamental concepts of GIS and then practice them on small but practical projects. For example, Niederhuber's course includes a GIS-based case study project that is within the context of environmental problem-solving and in collaboration with an outside organization. The outside organization proposes the case study topic, and with instructor guidance, the students are responsible for carrying out the project. The students plan the schedule, define the criteria for analysis, select relevant GIS data, create conceptual models and workflows, transform the models with ArcGIS, and present their results to the course plenum and external partner. In the past, students have worked with various partners, such as Swiss Regional Parks, and have completed projects such as modeling potential weasel or hazel grouse habitats.

Undergraduate students also participate in various biodiversity excursions. The excursions use a practical approach to encourage students to explore aspects of data literacy through real-world experiments. Using ArcGIS Collector, students as a group map large datasets on spatially relevant issues. The excursions serve to familiarize students with GIS, create interactive lessons, and encourage students to consider spatial information. Students have used the excursions to capture data on topics ranging from mapping trees, flowers, fungi, butterflies, tiger mosquito breeding spots, and birds to collecting wind speed and direction and tracking soil depth.

In addition to the undergraduate course instruction, Niederhuber teaches a graduate-level GIS course focused on spatial data analysis, modeling, and optimization. In this course, students use ArcGIS Online and ArcGIS Pro for 3D modeling and data analysis.

Niederhuber's GIS expertise goes beyond the classroom. For the last three years, she has led an established GIS user group for researchers. The group was founded 15 years ago and meets yearly to allow members to exchange ideas, present research, and help each other solve problems. "The goal was to bring together scientific assistants, PhD, and postdoctoral students working with ArcGIS to network, collaborate, and learn from one another," said Niederhuber.

Geospatial research's impact on the future

In the early days of the Institute of Cartography, primary research focused on topographical cartography (mapping of terrain), thematic cartography, and atlas cartography (school atlases, national atlases). In 2011, Martin Raubal joined ETHZ as a professor of geoinformation engineering, the institute's name was changed to the Institute of Cartography and Geoinformation, and a new era of education and research was ushered in.

"We utilize geoinformation and location-based data in many areas of our lives, whether public transportation, sustainability, or environmental protection. It would be a challenge to find an area or domain where GIS can't be applied," said Raubal.

Accordingly, Raubal encourages his students to consistently consider where to apply geoinformation and location data. This has led Raubal's geoinformation engineering research group to offer courses including elements of spatiotemporal machine learning and data science. Students not only learn about GIS-specific methods and applications of data science in neighboring fields but also apply them in their research projects.

Students study a wide range of topics such as analysis, simulation, and prediction of human mobility; user profiling; Mobile

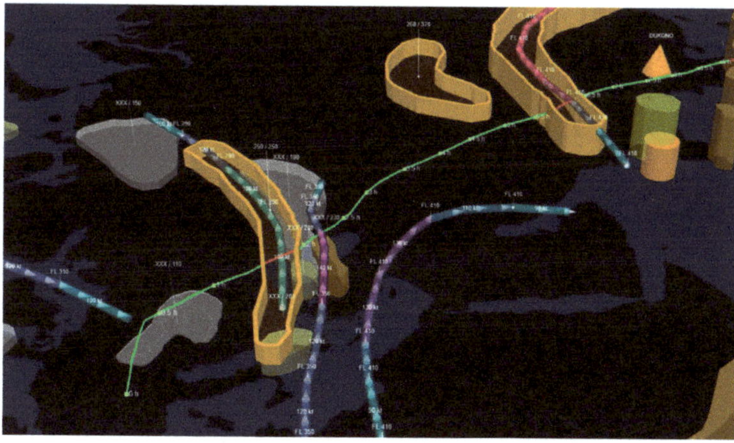

Turbulence ahead: A result of a master's thesis at ETH Zürich that visualizes aviation weather in 3D with the ArcGIS API for JavaScript™ 4.x for interactive exploration during preflight preparations by pilots.

GIS and location-based services; cognitive engineering for geospatial services; mobile eye-tracking to evaluate individual mobile decision-making; GIS for renewable energy analysis and prospecting; spatial cognition and wayfinding; time geography; and personalization. Many of these studies have used Esri technologies.

For Raubal, "GIS is broad, where no matter how we use it, it can be applied to many different real-world problems. But I think that GIS can be much broader, and I strongly believe the future is spatial data science, because spatial components are already so integral to everything we do."

Students have applied this mindset while conducting their research at the institute's two core labs, the Mobility Information Engineering Lab and geoGAZElab. For example, students leading the research on GIS for renewable energy have developed a GIS-based algorithm for the fields of biomass, solar, and wind energy to identify technically and economically exploitable potential for power generation. The students' research also considers the regulatory and economic frameworks for Switzerland to plan for transmission lines and determine locations for biomass power plants.

A thriving GIS partnership

Over the years, ETHZ has maintained a strong partnership with Esri, and the Institute of Cartography and Geoinformation has earned designation as an Esri Development Center (EDC). The distinction places the institute in an elite group of global ArcGIS users in education whose work goes beyond typical classroom use. Several students from the programs have been named EDC Student of the Year, an award given by Esri founder and president Jack Dangermond. Winners receive cash prizes, a certificate, and an Esri Press book and are invited to participate in the annual Esri User Conference in San Diego.

In 2017, Lisa Stähli won the Student of the Year award for her project, "Pedestrian Navigation in a Virtual Urban Environment: Evaluation of Wayfinding Directions Indicated on Public Displays." The master's-degree project investigated pedestrian navigation aids and aimed to find alternatives to the widely used map-based navigation systems. Using ArcGIS CityEngine® technology, Stähli created a virtual 3D urban model that was imported into Unity 3D, a game engine with added animation and interaction with the navigation systems. Using the created model, Stähli tested four navigation techniques with a group of 45 individuals, producing a valuable dataset and statistically proving that augmented reality was the best wayfinding tool.

A pair of students, Hasret Gümgümcü and Daniel Laumer, shared the Best Student prize in 2019 for the UrbanX project, a mixed-reality scenario app combining HoloLens and gesture recognition technology with city planning apps. The UrbanX app provides functionalities to assist urban planning initiatives.

In 2020, Samuel Küng from the Environmental Systems Science Department won the Esri Young Scholar Award with his master's thesis, "Deriving Forest Masks according to the Forest Definition of the Swiss National Forest Inventory Based on 3D Remote Sensing Data."

Students from ETHZ have also gone on to find successful careers in GIS and with Esri. For example, Stähli now works for the ArcGIS Urban team at the Esri R&D Center, Zurich AG. Christian Sailer, business development manager for education at Esri Schweiz (Switzerland) AG, completed his PhD in Raubal's geoinformation engineering group with a thesis focused on a mobile learning project, titled "OMLETH." The thesis focused on the development of a map-based learning platform for educational institutions, featuring multimedia field trips to create an authentic, location-based mobile learning experience. The OMLETH app bridges the gaps between GIS technologies and lesson management by assigning content lessons to spatial locations. This software is being used for augmented exercises for on-site work in research and is still in use at several secondary schools. OMLETH's clients are hosted on ETHZ's ArcGIS Online account because of its powerful cloud capabilities and ready-to-use user management.

"With ArcGIS Online, ETHZ has a tool that anyone can use quickly, doesn't require expertise, and displays data easily," said Sailer. "Thanks to this technology, students, researchers, and faculty can approach spatial challenges as efficiently as writing a report or calculating small statistics using MS [Microsoft] Word or MS Excel."

For now, ETHZ's robust education and research programs will continue to provide students with learning opportunities that contribute to the future of geoinformation and location-based sciences.

A version of this story originally appeared as "Building a Geospatial Legacy at the Swiss Federal Institute of Technology" on esri.com in 2021.

STUDENTS MAP INGENIOUS ROUTE TO CLEAN WATER

Saaf water

NEARLY ONE-THIRD OF THE WORLD'S POPULATION—MORE than 2 billion people—lack access to safe water. And nearly all of them have no way of knowing whether the life-sustaining liquid they draw from a village pump could kill them or make them deathly ill until it's too late.

But an enterprising group of young computer coders in India has created a low-cost system that can go a long way toward saving lives, preventing severe illness, and helping ensure that one of the most basic human needs—water—will not harm those who do not live near modern plumbing or have access to purification methods.

Chosen as the 2021 global winner of IBM's Call for Code contest, the system that can alert people to the likelihood of contamination in the water they depend on for drinking, cooking, and cleaning has gained worldwide attention. One mainstream news source in India said the group's invention could save millions of lives.

The need for a low-cost, easy-to-use water quality system seems obvious today, especially now that it has attracted the attention of coders and GIS users around the world. The first-place finish comes with a $200,000 prize and the promise of guiding expertise to help take the idea from proven prototype to widespread deployment as a working solution.

Although the system has been praised as an astonishingly simple and workable solution, it took a frightening event to compel the young coders and entrepreneurs to see the enormity of the problem and the urgency of the solution.

A mother's illness spurs invention that saves lives

When Hrishikesh Bhandari found out that his mother had become severely ill from contaminated water, it set in motion a journey of discovery that may ultimately relieve suffering and save many thousands of lives. Through simple water-testing devices, cloud-based data storage, and machine learning, the Saaf water group has created a way to alert people in neighborhoods and villages that the water they depend on may sicken them.

To make the data readily accessible and understandable to government entities and especially those who may be directly affected by tainted water, the group used GIS to plot data on maps and show contamination spots and areas likely to become health risks.

The GIS dashboard, along with color-coded and regularly updated smart maps, can keep residents aware of the quality of their drinking water in real time.

Do you know anyone else sickened by their source of water?

After thinking about his mother's illness, Bhandari checked with his friends to ask whether anyone close to them had also suffered after ingesting tainted water from their village or neighborhood's traditional source. He found water-related illness to be common. Everyone seemed to have a relative or friend who was sickened at some point by contaminated water.

Although parts of India are modern, many areas still suffer from a lack of drinkable water and the treatment services to make it safe. As a 2020 United Nations (UN) report notes, the issue of contaminated water is complicated by the fact that areas without modern plumbing and treated water also have poorly managed garbage and human waste disposal systems. In fact, the UN report notes that 3.1

billion people—or 46 percent of the world's population—live in areas that fall into this category.

In the case of Bhandari's mother, the doctors related her declining health to tainted water. It took three painful months for her to recover.

As the others in the group—Jay Aherkar, Satyam Prakash, Manikanta Chavvakula, and Sanket Marathe—did their research, they, too, were galvanized into action by what they found.

Bhandari said, "That's why we thought, 'Let's build a solution around this,' because it's not a problem that just we've encountered, but it is a problem that everybody is going to encounter in the future or is encountering currently."

Saaf water is born

As group members began to organize their thoughts and set up a plan to do something about the ongoing problem, they formed Saaf water. In Hindi, *saaf* means clean.

They decided that there had to be a way to help—an app or a device that could save lives, wouldn't cost a lot, and would be easy for the average person to understand and use. They realized that to be effective, their device and the system had to be simple to operate and understand and low cost to be within the reach of low-income communities.

They created a system with a light at the water source—green for safe, yellow for high likelihood of unsafe water, and red for warning of a confirmed contamination. The information and layers of data gathered from current and historical weather patterns, seasonal correlation, population growth, local farming methods, and commercial development reflect some of the trends affecting groundwater quality.

The goal of Saaf is to put the hardware-software system in the communities that need it as soon as feasibly possible. That's why

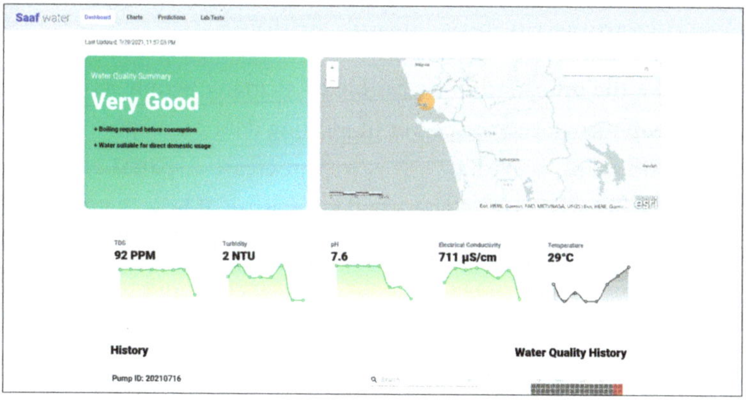

Saaf water dashboard showing very good quality water.

team members, although excited and humbled by their win, are also anxious to move into deployment and make good on their pledge to improve conditions for more than 2 billion people.

"My family felt proud," Marathe said. "For me, it's not about celebrating the win; it's about getting a long-term responsibility to apply things and to take things forward."

However, it's not just a lack of proper human waste disposal or industrial runoff that causes biological and chemical contamination. Climate change adds another layer of complexity.

"Because climate change is on the rise, what is happening is sea level is rising and penetrating into groundwater. This pattern increases salinity and bacterial contamination," Bhandari said.

After winning the IBM global challenge, the five have continued to refine their system. They are trying to collect data of all types, including historical weather patterns and current water quality. This data will help refine the algorithms that predict when chances of contamination are expected to increase. Warnings can be sent out to those in the area, and local governments can be alerted to begin more thorough water testing.

Visualizing the analysis through mapping

To make the information accessible to as many people as possible, the group recognized the power of plotting data on maps.

"With maps, what happens is we can create a spatial awareness system," Bhandari said. "Users will get a sense of how water quality spreads across the landscape."

That helps governments see the larger picture and trends in contamination. It also can help neighborhoods, communities, and even regions develop a bond over water needs that could translate into the political will to solve the problem. The Saaf water system also has the capacity to suggest treatment and prevention options based on what the electronic sensors detect in the water.

In addition to IBM resources, the group had assistance in creating maps that allow users to visualize trends and problems. "With Esri India's help recently, we have brought spatial awareness to a new level, which provides our users a sense of what's happening in their neighborhood," Bhandari said.

Although Bhandari's mother went through a terrible three months, she was proud that her son's project could save others from illness and death. "I didn't see her reaction in person," Bhandari said. "But from what I heard from her and my brother, she was literally crying when she heard that Saaf water had won."

A version of this story by Christa Campbell originally appeared as "Students in India Map Ingenious Route to Save People from Contaminated Water" on the Esri Blog on February 8, 2022.

STUDENTS SEE OPPORTUNITIES FOR COMMUNITY GROWTH

Penn State University

IN FALL 2020, STUDENTS FROM THE PENN STATE UNIVERSITY geodesign program participated in a studio project that focused on revitalizing the city of Utica, New York. During the project, they used ArcGIS technology to develop and present recommendations for the city to implement after the completion of its new hospital.

Penn State University offers geodesign graduate degree and certificate programs that empower the next generation of environmental and urban design experts around the world. The programs are offered entirely online and designed for working professionals.

Geodesign uses the analytic side of GIS technology for a dynamic approach to designing and planning land-based projects that are environmentally, economically, and socially sustainable. Students in the program hail from a variety of academic disciplines and different levels of GIS understanding. The goal of the three-year program is to develop students into creative problem solvers who understand and can orchestrate the process of geodesign.

Each year, the program offers students the opportunity to gain hands-on experience at studios in two settings: urban and rural. The urban design studio presents challenges and complexities that are common to revitalizing a city. In fall 2020, a blended cohort of graduate and undergraduate students collaborated over 14 weeks on a citywide revitalization project for the City of Utica, engendered by the city's plans to build a new hospital.

"We knew where the hospital location was, and we wanted to know what kind of effects [it would] have throughout the community. How can we look at the broader picture and opportunities for

The visualization on the left shows existing conditions in Utica, whereas the right shows modifications that would produce a safe, accessible city center that encourages walkability and bikeability. These changes would align improvements in Utica's downtown core with Utica's downtown revitalization initiative. (From an ArcGIS StoryMaps story by Sara Schwartz.)

community growth that this might bring?" said James Sipes, lecturer in geodesign at the Penn State Department of Landscape Architecture.

Sipes and his colleague Dan Meehan, Penn State geodesign program manager, consider it vital that students not only interact with innovative technology but also think about urban design and planning differently so that they can better use it.

Sipes and Meehan format class projects around the International Geodesign Collaboration (IGC) framework. In this case, using this format allowed students to study three design scenarios for the City of Utica: early adopter, late adopter, and the current business-as-usual trajectory.

When these scenarios were visualized, they highlighted the cumulative impact of implementing planning strategies sooner rather than later. To frame the problems or challenges they chose to study, students were asked to estimate the impact of their strategies on the UN Sustainable Development Goals. By using the IGC format, students could evaluate scenarios to see whether they positively or negatively affected sustainability goals. "The key point wasn't to have students reach every goal but to see how the changes they were proposing would impact different levels of sustainability," said Meehan.

GIS—specifically, ArcGIS Urban—helped students visualize these interconnected challenges and methods for resolving them. "ArcGIS Urban was at the core of what we were doing primarily because it's one of the few tools we know of that [would allow] us to put in so many different variables, assumptions, and different complexities at that scale and allow us to visualize the impacts," Sipes said. During the project, students used CityEngine, ArcGIS GeoPlanner[SM], ArcGIS Online, and ArcGIS StoryMaps[SM] in addition to Urban.

Some students needed help learning these tools, but Esri staff provided multiple training sessions as well as tech support. Graham Mills, who is pursuing a bachelor's degree in landscape architecture at Penn State, said support from Esri staff helped him learn the workflows and gain the skills and expertise he needed for his career.

The first half of the project focused on where the hospital would be located—the city's U-District, an area of downtown for small businesses and entertainment. This portion of the project helped students become familiar with the course concepts and tools on a small scale. The students' analysis included existing and potential business options, ideas to revitalize the historical character of downtown Utica, and opportunities to attract new residents.

"We went from this smaller-sized project to [saying], 'OK, now that you have reimagined what would happen there, now apply that to an entire city.' So, they had to stop and think about the things they had learned in that first project and apply it on a larger scale," Sipes said. "We wanted them to think big about how to change the entire city but think in a methodical way on how we can get there."

A central tenet of the geodesign approach is understanding key stakeholders. As a class, the geodesign students came up with five

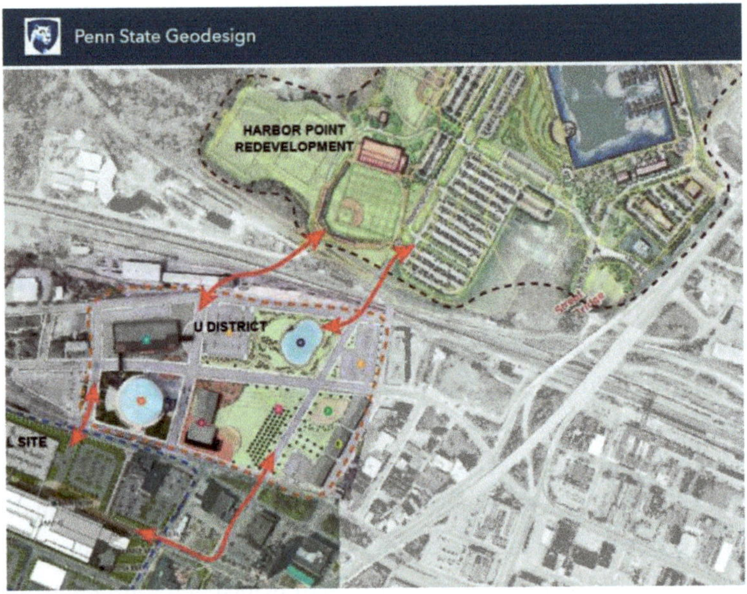

Analysis revealed lack of connectivity between multiple city master plans. (From an ArcGIS StoryMaps story by Leslie Hendricks.)

groups of stakeholders: government, residents, business owners, hospital affiliates, and developers. Acting as stakeholder group representatives, the students researched the needs and goals of each group.

They outlined a series of key topics including improving health and wellness with community gardens and agricultural farms, upgrading streets to be more pedestrian friendly, and working with new zoning plans and parcels. One project featured a tree-planting initiative that would focus on vacant land and parking lots to add greenery, enhance air quality, and improve wellness across the city.

"One of the things students did well was that they stopped thinking about singular issues and began to think about multiple issues and overlapping benefits or impacts," Sipes noted.

At the end of the course, students used Urban to present 3D

visualizations and massing models of all the buildings in Utica. They were able to model zoning changes, propose transportation networks and bike lanes, and map areas for parks and gardens. Students presented their findings to geodesign experts and Utica city staff, using ArcGIS StoryMaps stories to deliver information in a graphical and easy-to-understand format. Student work is also viewable for further learning purposes through the Penn State studio design hub. Through their efforts, students gained significant technical skills and a new way of understanding and applying geodesign.

"As a student who is used to small-scale, site-specific designs, moving toward a city-scale project was a huge challenge," said Sara Schwartz, who is pursuing a master's degree in landscape architecture and a geodesign certificate at Penn State. "Overall, these digital tools and their features and storytelling capabilities enhanced my work and experience."

Looking to the future, Meehan and Sipes hope the geodesign framework becomes more widely used. Geodesign empowers analysis for data-driven decision-making and inspires people to think differently about addressing complex, ever-changing issues, they said.

A version of this story by Cassandra Wagner originally appeared as "Penn State's Geodesign Students See Opportunities for Community Growth" in the Summer 2021 issue of *ArcUser*.

MAKING GIS A STATEWIDE INITIATIVE

West Virginia Department of Education

INCORPORATING GIS TECHNOLOGY IN K–12 EDUCATION has been a goal of the West Virginia Department of Education (WVDE) since it established a statewide education contract with Esri in 2009. Investment in teachers and teacher training was an early focus and led to successes in developing a core group of GIS-savvy educators.

The challenge

The goal of WVDE has always been to move from this core group of GIS-savvy educators to a statewide implementation of GIS as a tool for teaching and student engagement. WVDE has kept pace with improvements in Esri software and used each improvement to reach more and more educators. The success of the WVDE initiative is because of a strong commitment to educator training and support, recognizing that these are the keys to student success with GIS.

The solution

The challenges surrounding a statewide implementation of GIS in education are many, but solutions are possible. In West Virginia, broadening the reach was accomplished in several ways. Creating standards for a course in GIS that can count as a third high school science credit led to many schools wanting to offer the GIS course. Developing an online GIS course for teachers created a way for them to learn enough about GIS to start working with students. To assist in teaching GIS, teachers received reinforcement through professional development, electronic mailing list postings, one-on-one support, and state-created teaching materials—all of which broke down barriers to GIS implementation. Lastly, setting up an organizational

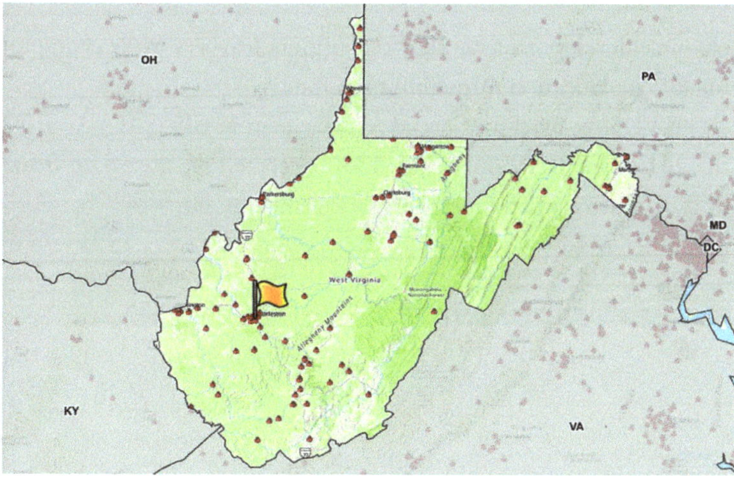

Each red dot represents a school in West Virginia that has an ArcGIS Schools Bundle of mapping software.

account for all West Virginia public school students and teachers, through single sign-on access, has enabled GIS across the state.

The results

WVDE educators and students now use ArcGIS Online for instruction and project creation. ArcGIS Pro is being used for administrative purposes and to create data layers for instruction. This initiative was run through the WVDE Division of Teaching and Learning, Office of Middle and Secondary Education, led by Executive Director Joey Wiseman. Since 2010, Erika Klose, a geologist and middle school science teacher, has been facilitating and coordinating GIS professional development for West Virginia educators.

Klose and Wiseman worked to provide training, access, and teaching resources for educators in all content areas, including career and technical education (CTE). Klose, now the STEM coordinator for WVDE, continues to provide GIS training, direct support, and resource development for all West Virginia teachers while championing GIS in education throughout the state.

WVDE received the Special Achievement in GIS (SAG) Award at the 2019 Esri User Conference. Klose accepted the award on behalf of the department and met with Jack Dangermond.

A version of this story originally appeared as "West Virginia Department of Education Makes GIS a Statewide Initiative" on esri.com in 2019.

HIGH SCHOOL HELPS STUDENTS EXPAND THEIR ANALYTIC CAPABILITIES

Loudoun Valley High School

AN INNOVATIVE PROGRAM THAT ALLOWS VIRGINIA HIGH school students to earn university credit for geospatial classes has been expanded to include a broader range of students.

The Geospatial Semester (GSS) is an innovative dual-enrollment program between high schools in Virginia and the Integrated Science and Technology department at James Madison University (JMU). Juniors and seniors are dual-enrollment students who take GIS classes at their high school and earn credit from the university.

Students learn how to find data, create maps, and apply mapping analysis tools to solve real-world problems. The GSS in Virginia is financially self-supporting (and has been for more than a decade).

Students from Loudoun County Public Schools (LCPS) participate in GSS. Loudoun County, located in the Commonwealth of Virginia, is part of the Washington, DC, metropolitan area. LCPS obtained an education license for Esri software more than 15 years ago. Today, geospatial science classes are taught in 11 of the county's 17 high schools.

Michael Wagner is the lead GIS teacher in the LCPS Science Office. "I developed the original GIS course with my colleague at Heritage High School, Jon Pruess," said Wagner. "We ran a pilot course for three years, and then started to roll it out to the other schools in the county." In addition to teaching earth science and geospatial science classes, Wagner oversees all geospatial science classes in the county and manages the district's relationship with JMU and GSS.

At the beginning of the 2019–2020 school year, Taryn Langmead,

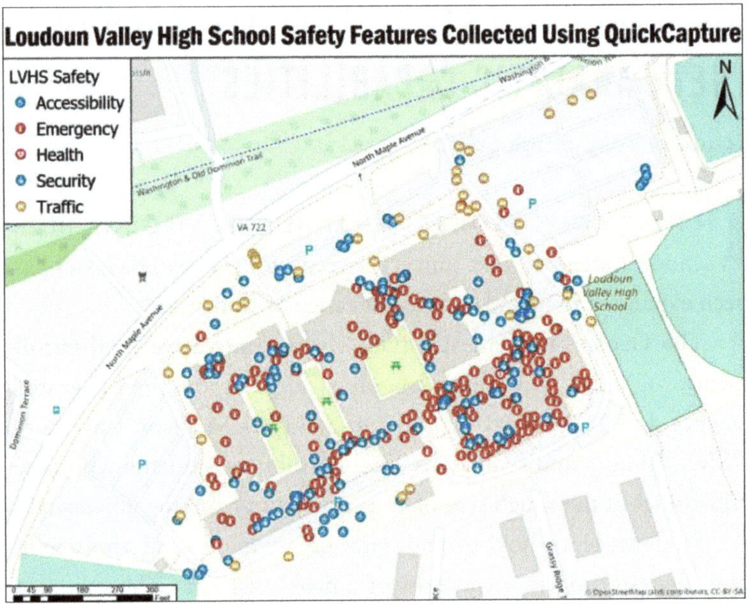

This map created by students shows the safety features located on the Loudoun Valley High School campus. Students collected the data for this map using ArcGIS QuickCapture.

earth science and geospatial science teacher at Loudoun Valley High School, teamed up with Dan Loper, special education teacher at the school, to teach a GIS class that combined exceptional learners with the dual-enrollment students.

"Basically, we decided to introduce geospatial science in the Basic Skills class for our exceptional learners that range from grade nine to returning graduates," said Langmead. The class was developed as a cooperative effort between the principal at Loudoun Valley High, the special education department chair, Loper, and Langmead. Support for class instruction was provided by teaching assistants Edwina Payne and Carrie Crum, as well as student helper Elsa Higbie.

"Foremost in our minds is how our exceptional learners have

just as much right to knowledge as their typically developing peers," said Loper. "Next, we considered differentiation. Our exceptional learners have diverse needs as individuals, sometimes changing on a day-to-day basis. We introduced the GIS concepts with those considerations in mind. These experiences may open doors for our students that might not have otherwise been available to them. In addition, the content may become an inspirational platform for our students to develop a love of the field and eventually find GIS employment."

"Dan had previously used GIS, so we were well equipped to scaffold GIS concepts to help the exceptional learners understand the expected outcomes for the class," said Langmead.

To make the course accessible to all students, descriptive teaching and learning techniques were adopted. Flash cards were used with some of the students to help them better understand GIS concepts and terminology. In addition, the course was referred to as geography science rather than geospatial science, and data was called number knowledge.

Lessons combine different approaches to learning content. For example, some lessons are computer based. Students use ArcGIS Online to complete them. In other lessons, students make models of the landforms they are studying.

Participation in projects varies to accommodate authentic inclusion and provide as much lesson detail and curriculum as possible. Projects can have many levels. For some projects, dual-enrollment students create maps and surveys using ArcGIS QuickCapture. Then these students work collaboratively with exceptional learners to gather data around the school campus. Exceptional learners enjoyed it when the dual-enrollment students worked with them on different projects.

Langmead built an augmented reality sandbox using information from the University of California, Davis (UC Davis). An augmented

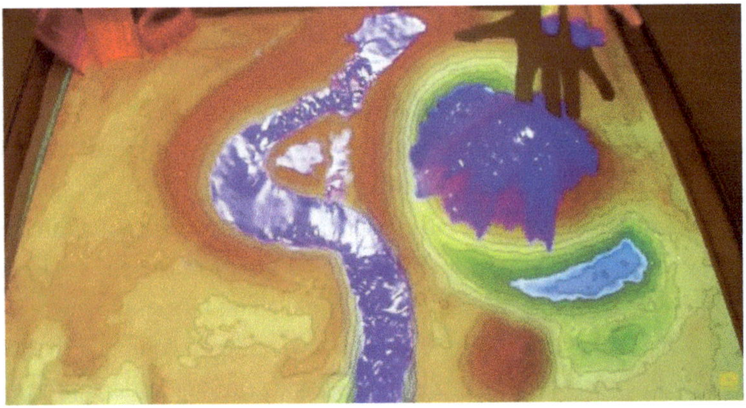

Teachers at Loudoun Valley High School built an augmented reality sandbox to teach earth science concepts in an engaging way using directions provided by the University of California, Davis.

reality sandbox combines sand with 3D visualization applications that were created through National Science Foundation-funded research at UC Davis. Molding the sand manually brings a simulated landscape to life. The visual perception of the sand is augmented in real time with a colored elevation map that has topographic contour lines and simulated water.

Loper and Langmead tried to place towns in the augmented reality sandbox as part of classroom lessons. Unfortunately, the COVID-19 pandemic curtailed their sandbox modeling activities, but the two teachers were able to continue using ArcGIS Online for data and visualization.

Exceptional learners provided perspectives that Loper and Langmead hadn't previously considered. They also had the opportunity to give the dual-enrollment students feedback on their midterm projects, which those students appreciated.

The teachers generally felt that taking the class helped the exceptional learners improve their communication skills because they

A student works on making a 3D relief of world topography after studying different maps and representations of the world using ArcGIS Online.

could better explain how they perceive the world. At the beginning of the school year, some exceptional learners were asked to provide details about a particular map feature, such as a mountain or a beach. Initially, students didn't know how to describe those features. As the school year progressed, however, these same students were making observations and analyzing what they were seeing on the map and connecting that with other experiences or information they had acquired.

"The students were enthusiastically engaged and often stepped up to challenges that were outside of their comfort zones. Some students would do really well with one task and then help out their classmates with the same task. Other times they would struggle, but there was always perseverance and encouragement fostered between all of the students," said Langmead.

"I think that the cognitive abilities among the students have most certainly improved at varying levels," said Loper. "This is evidenced by the demeanor in which they approach the class, the looks on their faces as they are getting to know various GIS concepts and tools, and the utter exuberance of some students as they embark on their GIS learning."

Wagner, the lead GIS teacher for LCPS, believes the spatial thinking skills these students develop will benefit them long after high school and might help them in getting a job that uses GIS.

"I would love to figure out a way that ArcGIS Online and some of the tools that come with it could be available to these students after high school," said Wagner. "I have worked with some of our job coaches on integrating the ArcGIS Workforce app for students who are involved in community-based instruction. Though we are in the early stages of this project, I believe it is a tool that can allow students to be more independent as they navigate daily tasks."

A version of this story originally appeared as "Virginia High School Helps More Students Expand Their Analytical Capabilities" in the Spring 2021 issue of *ArcNews*.

PART 2

RESEARCHERS

MODERN GIS TOOLS AND CONTENT SUPPORT YOUR research with fast access to authoritative data, robust analytic tools, and communication tools so that you can share results. GIS gives "superpowers" to a researcher, providing the ability to make sense of a large volume of data and data across different domains, increasingly in real time. GIS has moved away from being a niche technology to a platform that researchers across many fields can use, and in this way, it promotes interdisciplinary collaboration. Modern Web GIS integrates with many other scientific and engineering tools, such as R, TensorFlow, and scikit-learn. Leading researchers and scientists use GIS to advance the understanding of earth systems, human societies, and the interactions among them.

GIS provides researchers with a framework for creating knowledge through the following capacities:

- **Measure:** Combine and collect data from many sources.
- **Visualize:** Intuitively see patterns and trends.
- **Analyze:** Explore relationships for holistic understanding.
- **Evaluate:** Assess impacts and compare alternatives.
- **Communicate:** Share knowledge and inspire action.

Driven by research

GIS provides data integration, analysis, visualization, and storytelling capabilities that are uniquely engineered for data with a spatial component. Through collaboration with the research community, Esri constantly refines its tools to build on advances in theory and methods in spatial analysis, cartography and visualization, data science and computer science, and many other areas. Founded as Environmental Systems Research Institute, Esri spends about twice as much on research and development (R&D) as the average public company. Esri's 11 dedicated research centers around the world are at the leading edge of global innovation.

GIS in action

This section looks at real-life stories about how GIS enables, promotes, and expands research and furthers communicating that research to a greater number of researchers and policy makers across more domains. These examples include incorporating geospatial technology in what's known as "serious gaming" to help flood victims, examining the effects of land-use changes on water quality, evaluating campus tobacco use despite a university-wide ban, examining whether GIS in high school may cause physical changes in the brain, investigating past climate through ancient-tree studies, and studying habitat to save animal species at risk of extinction.

SERIOUS GAME PLAY

Rochester Institute of Technology

SITUATIONS SUCH AS THE COVID-19 PANDEMIC HAVE heightened interest in disaster management and mitigation. Researchers at Rochester Institute of Technology (RIT) in New York have used ArcGIS to create two serious games that can be important learning tools for responding to, mitigating, and recovering from calamities, ranging from hurricanes to pandemics.

In doing so, the researchers have tapped into a new trend—the gamification of GIS. One aspect is using location data and GIS technology to develop realistic, immersive 3D scenarios in the form of serious GIS games, or serious geogames, for training, science, and education. These games often use avatars, giving players a first-person perspective as they work through solving a problem.

A group of professors, cooperative-education students from RIT,

A volunteer, represented in the Project Lily Pad game by an avatar, tries to familiarize himself with a neighborhood in Dickinson, Texas. Dickinson suffered severe flooding during Hurricane Harvey in 2017.

and National Science Foundation (NSF)-funded college students from other universities across the country developed two serious geogames for disaster resilience research using open data and the 3D modeling software CityEngine. The games aim to teach general audiences, emergency managers, and first responders spatial thinking skills, and then use that knowledge to help communities withstand and recover from disasters.

"There is a lack of spatial thinking in the emergency practice right now, even though it can be really useful for identifying vulnerable populations, moving people to safe locations, and learning about how disasters impact areas," said Brian Tomaszewski, lab director of the Center for Geographic Information Science & Technology at RIT, who led the projects. "I think using gamification to make learning spatial thinking more engaging is a great way to get people thinking."

Games mimic real-life incidents

The serious games the team developed, called Project Lily Pad and Project EOC, are based on Hurricane Harvey, a Category 4 storm that battered Texas on August 25, 2017. Harvey caused catastrophic flooding, at least 68 deaths, and $125 billion in damage, according to the National Hurricane Center.

Research for the games began during two NSF-funded Research Experience for Undergraduates (REU) sites in GIS for Disaster Resilience Spatial Thinking. The REUs were hosted at RIT in the summers of 2018 and 2019 and led by Tomaszewski, who is also an associate professor in the School of Interactive Games and Media (IGM) at RIT.

The 15 students in the REU investigated maps, data, and survivor testimony to better understand the disaster. By combining elevation models and flood data, the group was able to create accurate 3D city models of Galveston County and Dickinson, Texas, to use in

Project Lily Pad simulates the scenario of using a boat to search for victims in a flooded neighborhood in Dickinson, Texas.

the games. Dickinson, which is in Galveston County, suffered major flooding and damage from Hurricane Harvey. The groups used GIS data from OpenStreetMap, along with Esri tools, to create their interactive maps.

ArcGIS Pro allowed the team to collect and process publicly available data from Galveston County, such as shapefiles of building footprints. After the datasets were processed in ArcGIS Pro, they were incorporated into CityEngine for 3D model development and eventual import into the Unity game engine.

In the game Project Lily Pad, players initially take on the role of a first responder in Dickinson. Players use a paper map to locate places to drop off supplies and navigate unfamiliar territory. Tomaszewski explained that during Hurricane Harvey, many of the National Guard members called in were new to the area, possibly making it harder for them to navigate the streets.

In day two of the game, the player's avatar is an informal volunteer from outside Dickinson who takes a boat through flooded streets

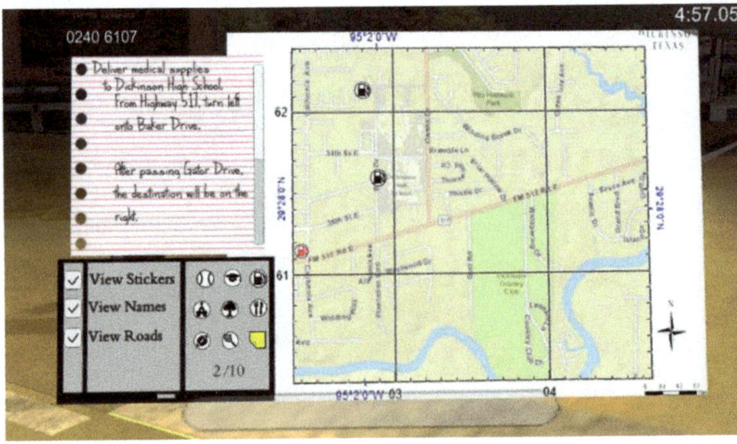

The first responders in the game use a paper map to find the locations to leave medical and other supplies.

to conduct search and rescue operations, much as the Cajun Navy (an informal volunteer group of private boat owners) did during Hurricane Harvey. Players must rescue people and drop them off at higher-elevation safe havens equipped with resources—locations that are known as lily pads.

"The term *lily pad* was actually used by first responders during Hurricane Harvey in Galveston County and was the inspiration for the game's name," Tomaszewski said.

The Project Lily Pad game helps volunteers and National Guard members—especially those coming in from other areas—familiarize themselves with the geography of the neighborhoods so they can respond more quickly when dropping off supplies or rescuing people.

"While responders are waiting to deploy at a disaster zone, they could play a game like this to familiarize themselves with the local environment," said Tomaszewski. "It's also useful for any audience, as it teaches spatial thinking skills with respect to flooding and hurricanes."

People are rescued from a flooded pickup truck during the game.

In the Project EOC game, players take on the role of an emergency operations center (EOC) manager in Galveston, Texas. As different disaster scenarios take effect, the player must make resource management decisions, including deploying ambulances, police, and firefighters, to control the situation. Project EOC was created using a combination of Esri tools including ArcGIS Pro for processing publicly available data that was then sent to CityEngine to create models for use in Unity.

In 2018 and 2019, members of the REU group traveled to Galveston County to collect field data that could be used in the game. They learned about how the hurricane impacted Dickinson, conducted interviews with survivors, and identified buildings that were still in need of repair. The group also worked with Galveston County Emergency Management professionals to conduct evaluation assessments of the games.

"We learned that this game could be a really useful supplement for the tabletop exercises that many EOCs do," said Tomaszewski.

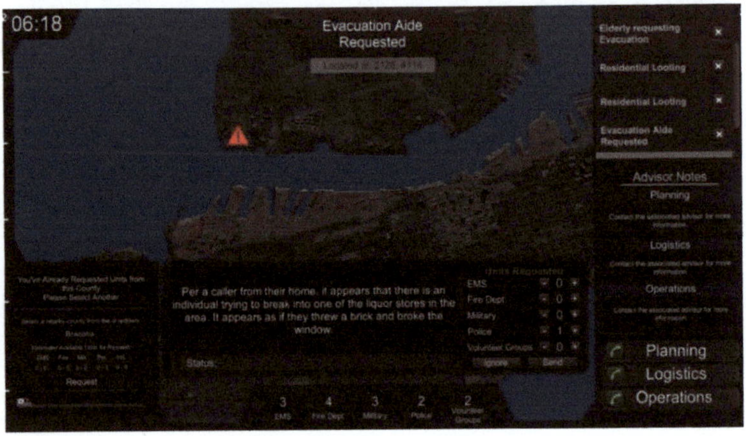

Project EOC, a game that trains players to respond to emergency situations.

"Having a virtual game could be more scalable, cost effective, and flexible for all of the people that are involved with these exercises."

Gamifying GIS data

With help from six RIT game design and development co-op students and David Schwartz, a professor and director of IGM, the geospatial data came to life as immersive, open source games.

Jeshua Johnson, a student at the University of Texas, Austin, who participated in the REU at RIT, was also part of the team that helped turn geospatial data into a 3D game environment. The process involved modeling the terrain and buildings and locating areas of interest for the game events, including the flood reports.

"Not many games are made with research as the focus," said Johnson, who is majoring in arts and entertainment technologies and minoring in geography. "Project EOC was an opportunity to approach games from a different perspective that has the potential to really benefit society."

The students started with GIS data from the Houston-Galveston

Students from several universities collaborated on developing the games.

Area Council, including building footprints, roads, and elevation data. After being imported into ArcGIS Pro, the data was edited to fit the area of interest for the project.

The data was then exported into CityEngine, where the procedural generation was used to generate 3D shapes, textures, and elevation.

"After initial generation of structures within the area of interest, we modified key structures throughout the area to better represent building heights in the Galveston/Texas City area," said Johnson. "These models were then exported as .fbx files to be imported into the Unity game engine."

The computer animation and modeling software Maya was used to create the building and character assets, which were then brought into Unity.

To design game play elements, the ArcGIS dataset was referred to again to correlate additional data related to flood reports and the locations of key infrastructure such as energy plants and hospitals.

"I was brought on to work on the underlying systems that

controlled game play, such as triggering disasters and tracking progress behind the scenes," said Alexander Amling, a third-year game design and development student at RIT. "I really enjoyed working on a research-driven, practical project alongside researchers with backgrounds that were very different from my own. I found the entire experience to be a great way to explore the more academic side of software development."

Project Lily Pad and Project EOC are free to play. You can download the games on GitHub or follow the instructions on the RIT Center for Geographic Information Science and Technology web page.

A version of this story by Scott Bureau originally appeared as "Serious Game Play" in the August 2020 issue of *ArcWatch*.

COMMUNITIES SEE HOW LAND-USE CHANGES MAY AFFECT LOCAL WATER QUALITY

Tipping Point Planner Program

NUTRIENT REDUCTION IN BODIES OF WATER IS A CRITICAL goal for communities in the United States, particularly in northern states that border the Great Lakes, where nutrient loads—high concentrations of pollutants such as nitrogen and phosphorus—threaten the health of rivers, tributaries, inland lakes, and bays. Communities often need to know the quality status of their watersheds and how development plans might affect it. Many questions arise during the planning process, such as the following:

- Are current nutrient loads impairing surface water quality?
- If we develop a particular site, would our streams or other bodies of surface water cross a critical threshold where they change from a healthy state to impaired?
- What mitigation management strategies are the most cost effective?

To answer these questions, communities need science-based tools that link planning decisions to water quality. These tools must be established within a framework that involves community organizations, natural resource experts, scientists, extension specialists from land- and sea-grant universities, and concerned citizens.

In 2006, a group of 22 scientists from nine institutions formed a coalition—the Tipping Point planning team—to promote and educate communities about the science of tipping points—the point at which an ecosystem shifts from healthy to unhealthy—and how it

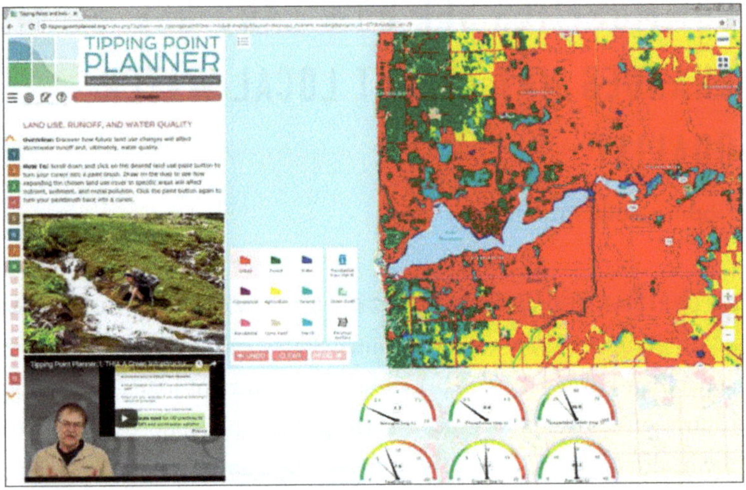

The Tipping Point Planner decision support tool helps program participants evaluate natural resources, prioritize community goals, assess changes, and explore what-if scenarios to come up with action plans.

relates to local watersheds. By combining GIS with the research outcomes of stream health, land-use change, and nutrient loading—and directly linking data to the local decision-making process—communities in the Great Lakes states can plan for a sustainable future.

The result of this partnership is the Tipping Point Planner Program, a facilitated workshop designed around a collaborative, web-based decision support tool that provides communities with information about local land use and watersheds in various multimedia formats. The interactive modules help participants do four things:

- Evaluate natural resource assets
- Prioritize community goals
- Assess past and potential future changes by displaying maps and gauges that indicate tipping point status
- Explore what-if scenarios with real-time models

At the end, the Tipping Point Planner generates an action plan that brings together these four items in a PDF, which contains maps, charts, and planning priorities.

GIS supports the science behind the decision-making tool

In this context, a tipping point is when an ecosystem shifts from a healthy state to an unhealthy state. A watershed in a healthy state typically contains a vibrant community of native fish species in clean water. When a watershed transitions to an unhealthy state, it is usually indicated by the mixture of native and invasive fish species in water that has potentially harmful algal blooms.

In Tipping Point Planner workshops, participants evaluate how proposed land-use changes might affect water quality in their communities. The online decision support tool integrates a variety of spatial models. Models include Purdue University's land-use forecast tool, Land Transformation Model (LTM); water quality tools such as Purdue's Long-Term Hydrologic Impact Analysis (L-THIA) model; the US Geological Survey (USGS) SPARROW (SPAtially Referenced Regression on Watershed attributes) model; and the University of Michigan's land-use biotic tipping point model, which provides the status of nutrients, sediments, fish, and aquatic insects in streams. Incorporating separate models such as these enables planners to analyze a range of plans over a period of two to five decades.

Additionally, the Tipping Point Planner's GIS-based tools allow you to visualize the results of the models on a map. You can zoom in and out and pan the map to see stream quality ratings at different spatial scales (e.g., local versus regional). The team also employed the National Hydrography Dataset with land-use classification to generate a seamless network of stream reaches and elevation-based catchments, which allows you to see how land drains into specific rivers or streams. And topical pages, which show information such as how to decrease nutrients or protect farmland, are modeled after ArcGIS StoryMaps, with a narrative pane on the left that guides you through using the decision support tool and a main stage on the right where you can interact with the map, data, and graphs.

The Tipping Point Planner in action

Many cities in the Great Lakes region need to improve their water quality. In Peoria, Illinois, for example, water surge from storms and melting snow often exceeds the capacity of existing storm water infrastructure, which results in sewer overflow and other excess nutrients polluting the Illinois River. As in many other communities, this has afflicted Peoria for years—to the point that both the United States and Illinois Environmental Protection Agencies (EPAs) have mandated that the city develop a plan to address the problem.

The City of Peoria and its innovation team organized a Tipping Point Planner Program workshop to explore solutions. An extension specialist from Purdue held an initial discussion with community leaders about their specific watershed problems, goals, and community engagement options. This facilitator also conducted a series of workshops that brought in Tipping Point planning team members who have specialties in community planning, GIS, public engagement, biology, and landscape modeling.

"Peoria has an issue they're trying to resolve before they cross the tipping point, and there are very costly solutions to it, but we're helping them explore alternatives that are less costly and would provide other environmental benefits as well," said Bernie Engel, professor of agricultural and biological engineering and associate dean of agricultural research and graduate education at Purdue University, who is leading the Peoria project.

The Tipping Point Planner Program helped Peoria's innovation team figure out not only what environmental variables needed

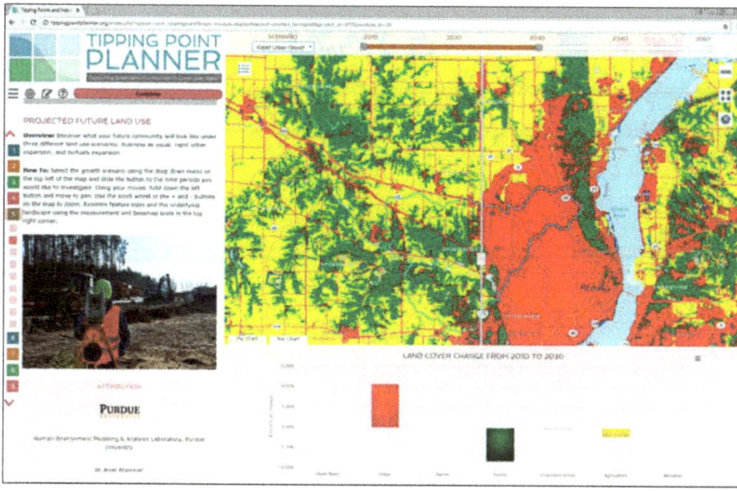

The City of Peoria, Illinois, uses the Tipping Point Planner Program to figure out how to mitigate sewer overflow and other excess nutrients polluting the Illinois River.

attention but also how to choose from a host of solutions based on model simulations of anticipated nutrient reductions and the costs of various remediation options. Using the decision support tool and a specific sewer flow model developed by Purdue's agricultural and biological engineering department, the City of Peoria got the guidance it needed to settle on a green infrastructure–based plan to address its sewer overflow problem. The plan, which the city is moving forward with, focuses on reducing impervious surface areas, such as pavement, and incorporating more porous surfaces into the community in the form of parks and open spaces.

Discovering tipping points before they can occur

Other communities are benefiting from the Tipping Point Planner Program as well.

To address the future of two watersheds near Saginaw Bay in

Lake Huron—the Au Gres River watershed and the East Branch Au Gres watershed—two Tipping Point planning team partner organizations, Michigan Sea Grant and Huron Pines, hosted a Tipping Point Planner workshop at Au Gres High School in July 2018. Over two days, community leaders, citizens, city planners, and natural resource professionals from the Saginaw Bay area took part in scientist-led group sessions and used interactive tools to explore three topics: green infrastructure, open space modeling, and nutrient modeling.

Workshop participants ended up discovering that their watersheds are in great condition but that they lack a plan to protect these largely unadulterated landscapes. Using the Tipping Point Planner modules, attendees identified priority areas for conservation.

Following the workshop, participants had access to the decision support tool and worked on generating a finalized action plan. A month later, the Tipping Point planning team hosted a follow-up workshop with the partner organizations to support their action planning efforts.

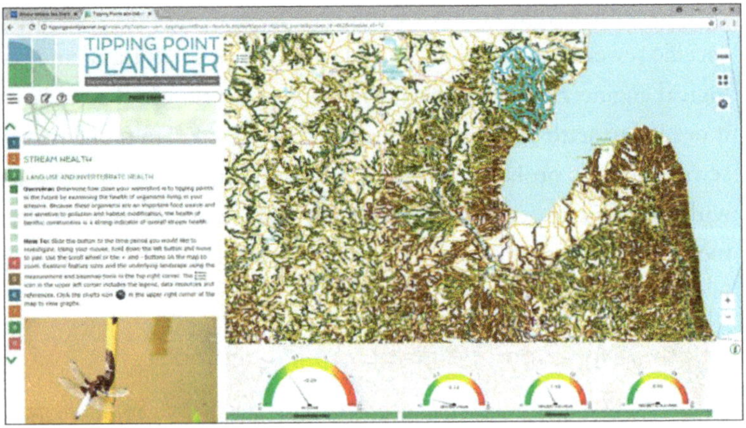

Michigan Sea Grant and Huron Pines found that two watersheds near Saginaw Bay in Lake Huron are in good condition but that local organizations need to come up with a plan to protect them in the future.

Technology expands to support an evolving project

As the use of spatial models in the planning process becomes more common, it is more important than ever to provide users with a variety of model outputs online—something the Tipping Point planning team is already doing and will continue to develop. This approach allows scientists and specialists to process more data using more sophisticated methods. Using an online platform could serve as a near real-time utility for the planning process in the future.

A version of this story by Kara Salazar, Lydia Utley, Bryan Pijanowski, Dan Walker, Jarrod Doucette, Kristen Bellisario, Brian Miller, Michael Wiley, and Ed Rutherford originally appeared as "With GIS, Communities See How Land-Use Changes May Affect Local Water Quality" in the Winter 2020 issue of *ArcNews*.

EVALUATING TOBACCO USE ON A TOBACCO-FREE CAMPUS

University of South Carolina

SELF-REPORTED SMOKING RATES AMONG COLLEGE students range from 9 to 25 percent, with rates in the United States highest among universities in the South. Studies show, however, that smoke-free restrictions in public buildings—including schools—have been associated with decreased rates of smoking in adolescents.

In 2009, the American College Health Association released a position statement recommending nine actions that colleges and universities should take to address tobacco policy, prevention, and cessation issues on campus, including strongly worded policies prohibiting tobacco use on all college and university property. Following these guidelines, the University of South Carolina (USC) in Columbia, South Carolina, implemented a campus-wide ban on all tobacco products, including e-cigarettes, in January 2014. The university announced its policy through the USC Healthy Carolina tobacco-free website, included references to the policy in student handbooks, and erected conspicuous signs around campus. The Carolina Community—which consists of students, faculty, staff, and volunteers—enforced the tobacco-free policy rather than university police or security.

Despite all these efforts, there were continued reports of tobacco use on campus. Seeing this as an opportunity to engage students in participatory research, a team of faculty and staff from several departments, together with several graduate and undergraduate students, set out to evaluate the presence of tobacco use at USC using GIS. The idea was to have students participate in all phases of the

Although the University of South Carolina is a tobacco-free campus, student volunteers recorded 24 tobacco-use violations during their 54 observation hours.

research, including designing the data collection forms they would use in ArcGIS Collector, gathering the locations of observed smoking violations, and mapping the data in ArcGIS Online.

Customizing Collector, and then gathering data

To get the project started, the team first customized Collector to record the appropriate information. In addition to being able to save the x,y coordinates of where individuals were observed using tobacco products on campus, GIS staff in the Department of Geography modified the app so it contained optional notes to record other variables, including whether there was more than one tobacco user in the area, the location's proximity to a no-smoking sign, the time of day, and any additional comments.

Once the app was ready to use, a group of trained student volunteers spent from October 2015 to March 2016 observing and recording tobacco use on USC's main campus. Using a weighted, random number generator (which focused on the center of campus, where there's greater population density), each volunteer was randomly assigned two locations on campus to monitor for 30-minute to 1-hour blocks of time, twice a week for 14 weeks. If they saw anyone smoking cigarettes, cigars, e-cigarettes, pipes, or hookahs, they used their own devices to record the tobacco-use violation in Collector. The app saved and pinned locations to the campus map in ArcGIS Online, where the team could then view and analyze the data.

Accruing and delivering valuable information

By the end of the observation period, student volunteers had completed 54 hours of observation time. They recorded 24 smoking violations—approximately one per every two hours of observation.

Of the 24 violations, 83 percent were lone smokers (versus smokers congregated in social groups). Nearly 17 percent of observed tobacco-use violations occurred within view of a no-smoking or tobacco-free campus policy sign. Also, approximately 13 percent of observed violators appeared to be external university contractors.

What surprised the team most was the abundance of cigarette and cigar butts found in some areas of campus compared with the relatively small number of smoking violations observed during data collection. This finding suggests that cleanup efforts are too infrequent or that violations often occur outside the observation window—at

Student volunteers observed an abundance of cigarette and cigar butts, prompting the study team to develop another customized Collector app to gather data on them.

night or on weekends. Based on these sightings, the study team subsequently developed another customized Collector app to gather data on cigarette and cigar butts.

Honing interventions

Using Collector and ArcGIS Online, the team at USC obtained the preliminary data it needed on where tobacco-use violations were occurring on campus. This data will enable the university to hone the smoking interventions it already has in place and perhaps come up with new ones. What's more, the students who participated in the project got to use GIS to collect and analyze real-world data, which they used to provide university administrators with valuable information.

A version of this story by Dr. Jan M. Eberth, Kevin Remington, Geoff Schwitzgebel, Jackie Knight, and Sarah Powell originally appeared as "Evaluating Tobacco Use on a Tobacco-Free Campus" in the Winter 2018 issue of *ArcNews*.

GEOSPATIAL BRAINPOWER: RESEARCH ON SPATIAL REASONING

The Geospatial Semester at James Madison University

A GROUP OF RESEARCHERS FROM SIX AMERICAN universities is studying what effect a classroom-based spatial education has on the development of the spatial thinking and reasoning skills of high school students. The research team wants to find out how the students, who use GIS technology for class projects, go about solving complex reasoning problems and whether their brains are physically changing in response to spatial learning.

With more emphasis on STEM courses in the American secondary school curriculum, an increasing number of students want to pursue STEM degrees at universities and, with them, the well-paying careers available on graduation.

Yet the anticipated success rate at universities for most of these students is low. According to ACT, the developer of a major standardized achievement test for college admissions, about half of the more than 2 million high school seniors who annually take the ACT placement test express interest in pursuing a STEM major. However, ACT test results indicate that only about 20 percent, or 200,000, of those students are academically prepared for the rigorous coursework required.

Although spatial reasoning and analysis are frequently applied in careers that fall under the STEM umbrella, these important skill sets aren't formally included in the secondary school curriculum. Instead, they are introduced incidentally in STEM-related classes when students encounter spatial concepts in the assignments.

Although many factors contribute to academic success, spatial reasoning is an overarching skill that could increase students' comprehension of STEM subjects if introduced during their secondary school years.

"Spatial thinking plays a very important role in the learning and practice of STEM-related disciplines," said Bob Kolvoord, dean of the College of Integrated Science and Engineering at James Madison University (JMU) in Harrisonburg, Virginia. "Many of the most important discoveries in science involved a critical spatial insight, such as the structure of the benzene ring or the DNA molecule."

The Geospatial Semester

One way to teach high school students spatial reasoning and help them retain those skills is to add GIS coursework to the curriculum. Broadly speaking, spatial reasoning covers all thinking that has a spatial component. This includes geospatial reasoning, which is geographic in nature. Spatial analytics methodologies often include the examination of physical features, such as the respective size, shape, and position of the objects or sites being studied and how they interact with nearby elements in their environment.

To help introduce students to spatial reasoning, Kolvoord cofounded the Geospatial Semester (GSS) in 2005 with his colleague Kathryn Keranen, an adjunct professor at JMU. Kolvoord and Keranen are also coauthors of several Esri Press books.

The GSS program offers high school juniors and seniors the opportunity to take GIS classes at their own schools while earning university credit at JMU. The program started at four high schools in Virginia but has expanded to include 30 high schools in Virginia, Oregon, and Illinois.

"We wanted to develop an educational program that exposed students to more problem-based learning through projects that require collaboration, and the use of GIS in their coursework was a good fit," said Kolvoord. More than 4,000 students have participated in

Two students who were recently enrolled in the Geospatial Semester observe final projects at a National Geospatial-Intelligence Agency (NGA) forum.

GSS thus far. Past student projects have explored a variety of issues related to the environment, renewable energy, wildlife, transportation, and public safety.

An analytic methodology for spatial cognition

Postulating that the students who participated in GSS had increased their spatial reasoning abilities, Kolvoord assembled a team to study whether exposure to GIS changes students' high-level STEM spatial thinking ability. The team developed testing procedures to determine how these changes occur at both the cognitive and neurological levels.

Kolvoord's chief collaborator on the team is David Uttal, professor of psychology and education at Northwestern University, where he works in spatial thinking in STEM education. Other members include Adam E. Green, an associate professor of psychology at Georgetown University who specializes in cognitive neuroscience; David Kraemer, associate professor of education in the Department of Psychological and Brain Sciences at Dartmouth College; and Emily Grossnickle Peterson, an assistant professor in the School of Education at American University, along with graduate students at all four institutions. Nora Newcombe, a professor of psychology at Temple University and former principal investigator at the school's Center for Spatial Intelligence and Learning, advises the team.

Kolvoord said that his and Uttal's approach to the research has evolved over the last 10 years. They started by interviewing students and assessing their final class projects. Students have used GIS to study a wide range of topics, including elk habitats, hurricanes, air quality in relation to California wildfires, and even school locker usage. The students primarily use ArcGIS Desktop applications in their coursework, but they use ArcGIS Online, too, when needed.

"We initially found that the GIS students used more spatial language and exhibited stronger problem-solving skills than other students," Kolvoord said. "We then added other collaborators to [our] team to more fully examine how the cognitive and behavioral aspects of the testing results connect."

The researchers explored the students' spatial thinking abilities, using standard psychometric measures. These include the mental rotation test (MRT), in which a person—selecting from a series of options—matches the shape of one figure to another figure by mentally rotating them, and the embedded figures test (EFT), in which the test taker recognizes geometric shapes from a bigger and more complex image.

Also, the students were interviewed and asked to answer a variety of questions: Why do you think gas or milk prices differ from gallon to gallon or brand to brand? How would you predict what the price would be for each gallon or brand? If you were trying to increase recycling in your community or to run for a local political office, how would you go about running your campaign?

"There are both spatial and nonspatial ways to solve these problems. By analyzing their answers, we examined both their use of spatial language and their problem-solving abilities," Kolvoord said. "We have ways to tease apart the interviews to look at how the students identify a problem, how they reason with the data, how they draw a conclusion, how they cite spatial data, and how they cite spatial representation. And the data we are collecting is really, really interesting. We have found that the open-ended problem-solving capabilities achieved by the GSS students seem to be making a difference in the development of their cognitive abilities that we can quantify."

The research also includes performing neuroimaging of the brains of students in the study groups, using functional magnetic resonance imaging (fMRI) technology. These tests determine whether physical changes in the brain occur with spatial learning, according to Kolvoord. "This allows us to develop biological inferences about how these changes occur and explain the effects of spatial education on core spatial abilities as well as high-level spatial thinking," he said.

Grants from the NSF and the Center for Spatial Intelligence and Learning support the team's work.

Kolvoord said the research he and other team members are doing is bridging a critical gap between the analytic work being performed in the cognitive neuroscience laboratory and its real-world applications in the classroom. Testing students provides the researchers with definitive, real-world data on what improves spatial cognition.

"More than two decades of research on how the brain performs spatial cognition has provided us with a reasonably clear understanding of the process," he said. "Our longtime, active engagement with those schools that teach the Geospatial Semester gives us access to a group of students exposed to a unique form of STEM education that is deliberately designed around spatial thinking and reasoning.

Because of our access to these students, we believe that this may be the first research that employs longitudinal data analysis to measure how learning in a real-world high school changes the brain."

What researchers have learned so far

The study included a test group of 79 students who had experience in learning and using GIS technology and a control group of 130 students who hadn't enrolled in GSS. Pre- and posttest data was collected on all 209 students, who came from both urban and suburban school districts and were demographically diverse.

"What we are examining in the behavioral interviews is the transfer of learning results," said Kolvoord. "This is the mental process in which past experiences affect learning and how it is used when we encounter a new situation. We're finding that students in GSS improve to a greater degree in the transfer of learning than students in the comparison group, suggesting that the use of GIS results in more than just procedural knowledge about a piece of software."

Analysis of the fMRI scans continues since the process is time consuming, Kolvoord said.

So far, the scan results have shown a significant effect when the GSS students mentally processed the embedded figures task.

"Specifically, there were differences in activation in the parietal region of the brain, which is related to spatial reasoning," Kolvoord said. "Students who took GSS had a greater blood flow in this region from pretest to posttest compared to the control group, implying greater activation."

Now that this part of the analysis has been completed for all students participating in the tests, researchers feel optimistic about the results. They haven't yet found whether there is increased white matter connectivity in the brains of the GSS students, but the researchers plan to continue work on that aspect of the project.

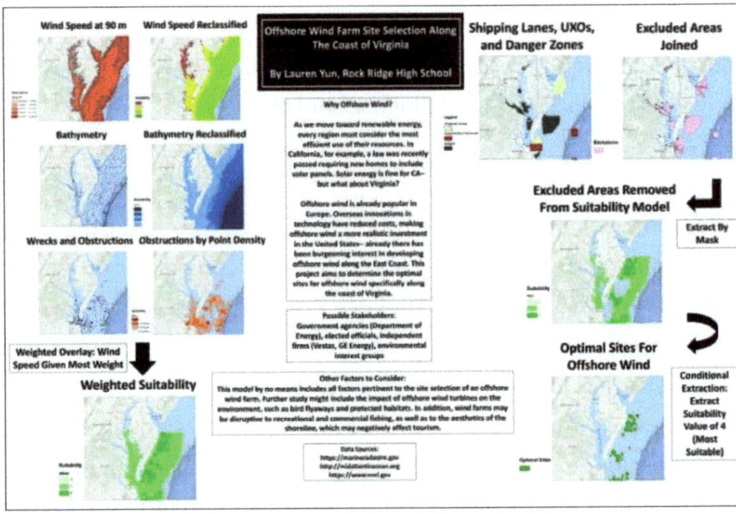

Lauren Yun from Rock Ridge High School in Virginia won a GSS award for her offshore wind project.

"While we have not completed the final analysis of all of our test results, we see differential improvement in the GIS students [compared to the control group] on STEM problem-solving skills, including problem definition and arguing from evidence," Kolvoord said. "These abilities apply broadly across STEM and other disciplines, as they are the key skills in critical thinking."

The research team will conduct a second series of experiments to determine the duration of GIS instruction needed to improve cognitive reasoning abilities.

A version of this story by Jim Baumann originally appeared as "Geospatial Brain Power" in the October 2019 issue of *ArcWatch*.

GIS AND ANCIENT TREES REVEAL PAST TEMPERATURES AND CLIMATE CHANGE

University of Arizona's Laboratory of Tree-Ring Research and Western Washington University

WALKING AMONG LIVING TREES THAT HAVE STOOD ON the side of a mountain since the times of Christ and Buddha is a humbling experience. In the White Mountains of California, ancient bristlecone pines grow to about two miles above sea level; above that, the weather is too harsh for trees to thrive or even survive. Many of these trees are more than 3,000 years old and have survived in an intensely harsh climate that is very dry, very cold, and very windy. The slopes are rocky and steep. The topography is complex. There is almost no vegetation—just rocks and sand underfoot. Ecologist Edmund Schulman called this feat of survival "longevity under adversity."

These trees, and others like them, represent an opportunity to unravel a problem: How do we better understand what the climate was like in the times before instrumental records? Some ancient trees can be considered the rain gauges and thermometers of the past. The annual layers of growth (tree rings) exhibited by trees are influenced by the environmental conditions during their formation. Evidence shows that tree-ring width in dry regions can provide a first approximation of the total rainfall over an interval of many months. In the high northern latitudes and in alpine tree line ecosystems, tree-ring width most closely approximates summer temperature. And yet, trees are not rain gauges, nor are they thermometers. Trees are biologic organisms potentially subject to the influence of multiple environmental and biologic factors that affect their growth during their lifetimes. It is the job of dendrochronologists (dendro means tree, and chronology means time) to interpret these growth records.

Work done at several universities, most notably at the University of Arizona's Laboratory of Tree-Ring Research, over the last 50 years has shown that the growth of ancient bristlecone pines (*Pinus longaeva*) at the highest elevations in the mountain ranges of the Great Basin in western North America is sensitive to temperature. The Great Basin is the largest endorheic watershed in North America. It spans portions of Nevada, Oregon, Utah, California, Idaho, Wyoming, and Baja California in Mexico. Over the past few decades, researchers have become more interested in which individual trees are most sensitive to temperature and how a spatial approach can improve understanding. For instance, using ArcGIS, research has shown that the position of the trees themselves on the mountainside has fluctuated up and down the mountain slope as temperatures have changed over the last several thousand years. There are stands of dead, twisted, and gnarled trees rooted in the ground more than 100 meters above the current tree line. These dead trees are reminders that the earth's climate is dynamic. They were alive during a period called the Holocene climatic optimum—a warm period that lasted from about 9,000 to about 5,000 years ago. The climate then was more suitable for these high-elevation trees (summers were warmer), and the tree line was higher than it is today. As the earth's orbit changed over thousands of years, the climate cooled, and those trees eventually died. However, these mountains are so dry and cold, and the bristlecone pinewood is so tough, that the wood has remained on the landscape for thousands of years. The record of growth in those rings speaks volumes about how climate has changed in the past and how it might change in the future.

Dendrochronologists strive to develop the best possible tree-ring chronologies of year-to-year changes in temperature obtainable from ancient bristlecone pine. For these regions, meteorological records of temperature from actual thermometers are available for roughly only the past century. A much longer time frame is required to adequately

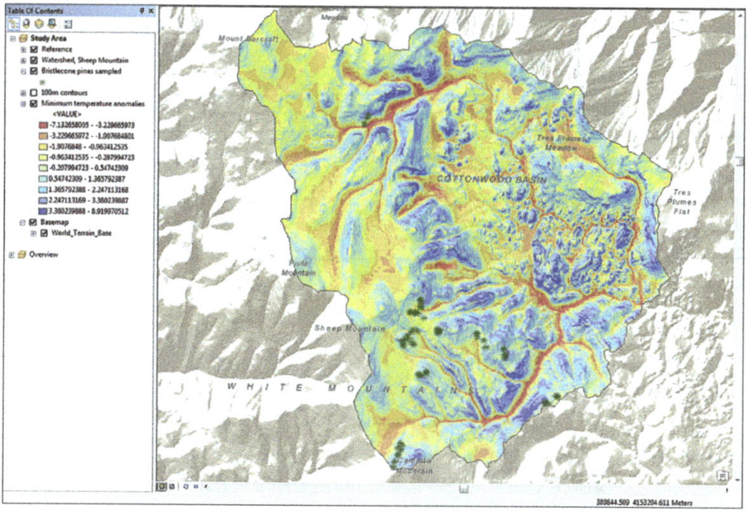

Minimum-temperature anomalies are derived using topographic indexes in conjunction with temperatures that loggers have arrayed over a rugged mountain landscape. These anomalies can be used to understand the microclimates experienced by individual trees.

understand the evolution of the earth's climate. By using the bristlecone pine chronologies as a proxy record of temperature, tree-ring scientists can better understand how variable the earth's climate has been over several millennia and test climatic theories and output from climatic models that many view as important for the future sustainability of modern society.

For decades, dendrochronologists have been working with the long bristlecone pine record to infer variability in past temperatures: if you can build a mathematical model relating current climate and tree growth, you can apply that model back in time and determine the climate. But the challenge is in knowing exactly which climate variables limit a tree's growth. As the botanical and ecological literature can attest, cambial growth (tree-ring width) in high-elevation trees is a complex biologic process. Thus, the most appropriate trees must be selected for field sampling—trees whose annual growth rings

This ancient bristlecone pine growing near the top of Mount Washington in the Snake Range in Nevada is near the upper elevational limit of growth for the species. The ring-width records of such trees reflect past variability in temperature.

will reflect variability in past temperature rather than, say, variability in growing-season soil moisture. The advent of precision GPS and detailed elevation models helps determine which trees are the best temperature recorders based on their precise location.

GIS technology can help determine the climate conditions that individual trees experience in these rugged and complex mountain environments. For example, micrometeorological models of temperature anomalies from cold air pooling, solar radiation models (such as the Solar Radiation toolset in ArcGIS) that take topographic shading into account, and remotely sensed information on the timing and

Tree rings are produced annually as large thin-walled cells that grow during the early part of the growing season, followed by smaller cells with thicker walls as the end of the season nears. The ring boundary is the abrupt change in cell size from the small thick-walled dark cells to the large cells formed at the beginning of the next growing season. In this image, the direction of growth is left to right, and the large openings are resin ducts. Note that some annual rings are relatively narrow, and some are relatively wide; this is the result of different climatic conditions encountered during the growing season.

direction of water from snowmelt can all be used to determine the physiological factors that limit tree growth. More specifically, combining data from inexpensive temperature loggers deployed on the mountainside with the hydrologic modeling tools in the ArcGIS Spatial Analyst™ extension shows that individual trees are experiencing variations in minimum daytime temperatures of several degrees in the summer. A tree growing in a colder microclimate resulting from cold air draining down the mountain might be more limited by temperature than one of its neighbors growing only a few meters away

This large dead bristlecone pine in the White Mountains of California stands at over 11,500 feet above sea level, above the tree line. The ring series sampled from this tree dates from 663 BC to AD 1024.

if that neighbor is located on a patch of ground that is relatively warmer. Indeed, the ring widths of trees growing on the same mountain slope vary in conjunction with their biophysical setting in predictable and measurable ways.

Determining exactly which climate variables were limiting growth was not possible at such a fine scale before dendrochronologists began to exploit the power of geospatial data. Now that these tools are becoming easier to use, the collaboration between those who are interested in time and those who are interested in space is poised to move the field of paleoclimatology onto firmer, clearer ground.

A version of this story by Matthew Salzer and Andy Bunn originally appeared as "GIS and Ancient Trees Reveal Past Temperatures and Climate Change" in the Winter 2013 issue of *ArcNews*.

MAPPING PIKAS' HABITAT TO HELP SAVE THEM

Nevada Department of Wildlife; University of Nevada, Reno; and San José State University

A TEAM DRAWN FROM THE NEVADA DEPARTMENT OF Wildlife (NDOW), San José State University, and University of Nevada, Reno, used high-resolution imagery, ArcGIS, and R to identify the habitat necessary for the survival of a species of small mammal that is sensitive to increasing temperatures caused by climate change.

American pikas (*Ochotona princeps*) are small mammals that inhabit fractured rock habitats, such as boulder fields and talus patches, at high elevations in western North America. Although pikas tend to inhabit high-elevation areas above the tree line, these thermally sensitive creatures have been affected by warming global temperatures, which has led to local extinctions and population declines over large parts of their range, particularly within the Great Basin ecoregion. In 2007, a petition was made to list pikas under the Endangered Species Act.

Recently, several populations of pika have been discovered at altitudes between 5,800 and 7,000 feet, relatively low elevations for the Great Basin desert in northwest Nevada. These pikas inhabit climatic conditions that are much hotter and drier than those of their Alpine relatives in other parts of the western United States.

These areas are large basaltic talus fields that are located across northwest Nevada as well as neighboring California, Oregon, and Idaho. The term talus describes rock fragments, usually coarse and irregular, that accumulate at the base of a cliff, chute, or slope. Talus environments allow pika to experience more moderate temperatures that are cooler in summer and warmer in winter. Although similar

The American pika inhabits talus fields usually at high elevations and is sensitive to changing temperatures.

talus areas exist through much of the landscape of northwest Nevada, many of these sites are not currently occupied by pika. Known occurrences of pika are scattered, and many recently discovered populations appear to have been wiped out.

To understand and catalog the occurrence of pika, the NDOW, San José State University, and University of Nevada, Reno, teamed up to create the Northwest Nevada Talus Atlas, the first talus atlas for the region.

Although not all talus patches are occupied by pika, talus is necessary for pika to persist. Having a good map of talus can help biologists plan field surveys in a systematic manner to ensure that no locations are left out. Mapping talus locations can also be used to understand how pika populations might be connected and how dispersal and gene flow might have occurred in the past and be occurring now.

The research team used maps of talus that were hand digitized from the Sheldon National Wildlife Refuge in Winnemucca, Nevada, along with imagery from the National Agriculture Imagery Program (NAIP). NAIP imagery is produced by the US Department of Agriculture Farm Service Agency. The team used imagery from 2017 that included red, green, blue, and near-infrared spectral bands and was resampled from 1-meter resolution to 5-meter resolution to speed processing. Using the polygons from the Sheldon National Wildlife Refuge study, the team generated 2,000 random points within talus areas and 2,000 random points outside digitized talus areas and extracted blue, green, red, and near-infrared reflectance from the NAIP imagery.

With this point data, the team calculated the Normalized Difference Vegetation Index (NDVI), Green-Red Vegetation Index (GRVI), and a pseudo albedo from the spectral bands. Using the Marine Geospatial Ecology Tools for ArcGIS, the team could access advanced machine learning classification tools through the R statistical computing language.

The Marine Geospatial Ecology Tools, a free open source geoprocessing toolbox that plugs into ArcGIS, was developed by Duke University to integrate ArcMap and R using Python and C++. It provides a user-friendly graphic user interface (GUI) that eliminates the need to know R code.

The team used the randomForest package for R, which implements a machine learning method for classification and regression known for its high accuracy, ease of use, and advanced graphing capabilities. The use of this package resulted in a classified map that had an accuracy rate of greater than 71 percent.

The extreme northwest portion of Nevada was not being classified as accurately in areas in which talus fields were intermingled with juniper woodlands. For this area, the team developed a separate classification by hand digitizing 1,172 talus points and matching them with an equal number of digitized nontalus points. The two

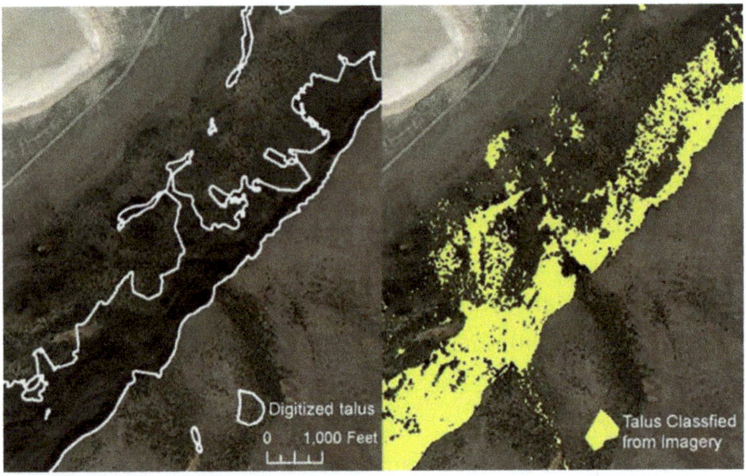

Maps show the digitized polygons (left) used to train the random forest classification model (right).

classified maps were combined, so the separately classified woodland map was used for the woodland portions, and the regular classification map was used in all other portions of the study area.

The research team made the Northwest Nevada Talus Atlas available through ArcGIS Online so that the data would be accessible to biologists in all parts of Nevada and the neighboring states in an easy-to-use format. The University of Nevada has a partnership with Esri that provides a certain number of credits to faculty, staff, and students for hosting their projects in ArcGIS Online. To ensure the maps displayed rapidly and smoothly, they were generalized at three spatial scales as tile services in ArcGIS Online. The underlying spatial data was made available as shapefiles for four subsets of the study area.

The research team plans to use the Northwest Nevada Talus Atlas to identify new field sites for future visits and understand how proximity to other talus patches and patch size influence the

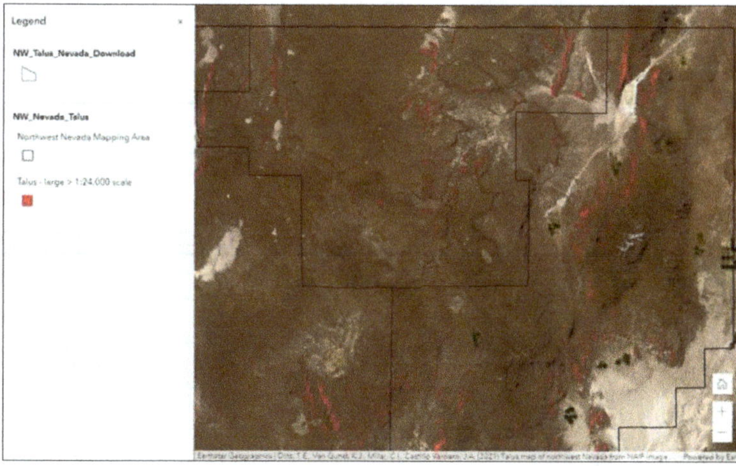

The Northwest Nevada Talus Atlas shows the location of talus fields within northwest Nevada. Data from the atlas is freely available in ArcGIS Online.

probability of pika persistence. The team is using climatic variables, vegetation indexes, and connectivity to determine whether sites where pika populations have recently ceased to be viable are in hotter and drier conditions or are more distant from neighboring talus.

To promote the viability of pika populations, biologists are also collecting genetic samples to identify which pika populations are most closely related, which are most isolated, and which are most at risk of population decline. In addition, biologists are using radiocarbon dating to estimate the time frames and patterns of the demise of pika populations across the region. Finally, NDOW works with the Bureau of Land Management (BLM), the regional land management agency, to identify threats to pikas, such as those from wildfire and livestock grazing, that may affect their food sources.

A version of this story by Thomas Dilts, Jane Van Gunst, and Jessica Castillo Vardaro originally appeared as "Mapping Pikas' Habitat to Help Save Them" in the Summer 2021 issue of *ArcUser*.

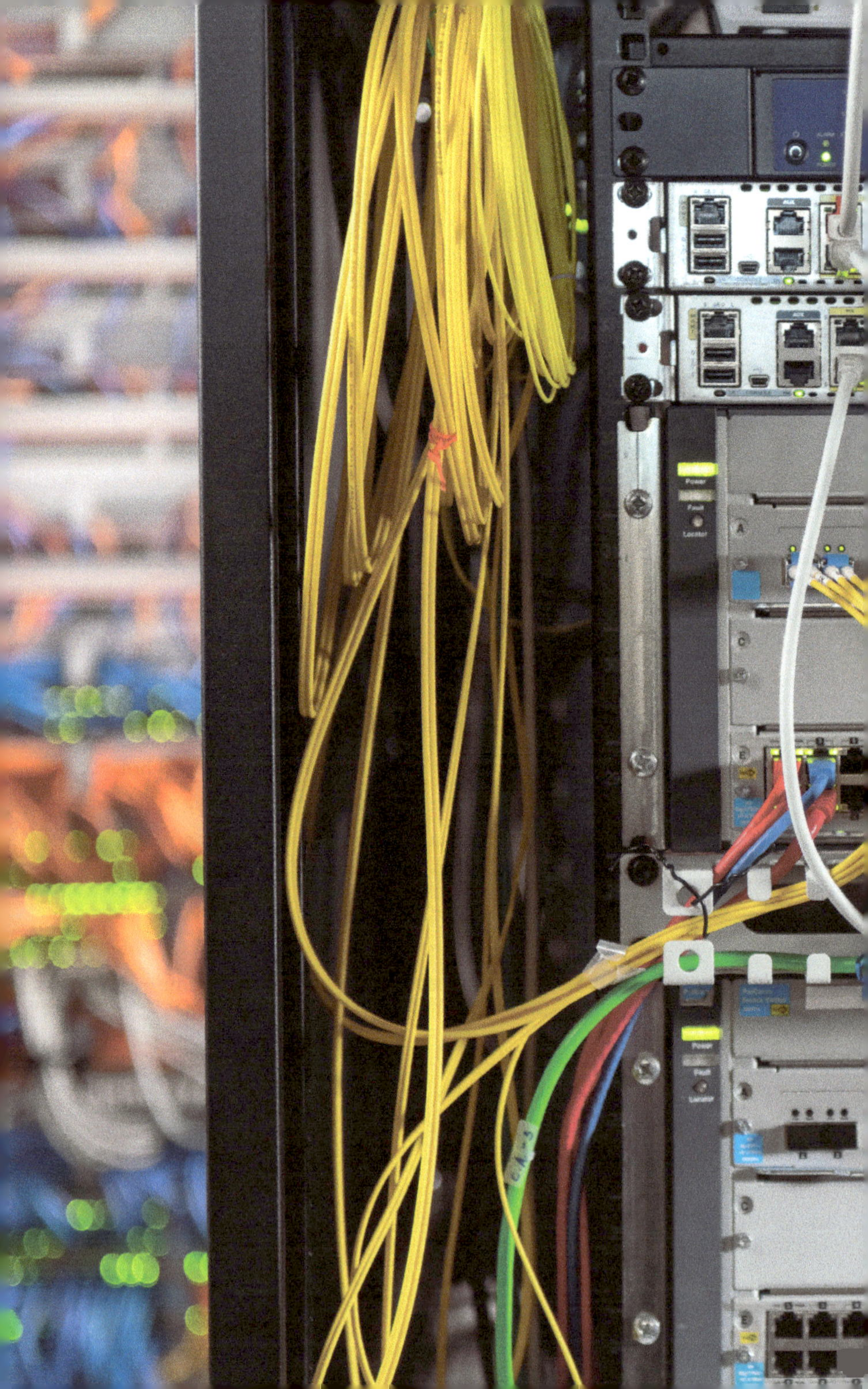

PART 3

IT SUPPORT

SCHOLARS IN DOZENS OF FIELDS USE DATA VISUALIZAtion and analysis tools. You can maximize the return on your technology investments with an integrated GIS suite that supports teaching and research in a wide range of disciplines, including the geosciences, social sciences, natural resource management, urban planning, business, and the humanities. From simple web maps to sophisticated analyses, GIS provides a common toolset for use throughout your institution. This reduces the learning curve for students and faculty, simplifies help desk inquiries, encourages collaboration, and streamlines management of information technology (IT) infrastructure.

GIS is a key piece of your institution's infrastructure

Enable access to data mapping and spatial data science tools throughout your institution with enterprise licensing backed by support and training and best practices shared by your peers. GIS provides institution-wide access to visualization, analysis, and collaboration tools that interoperate with your existing learning technologies and business systems.

GIS features that support enterprise-wide mapping and data visualization include the following:

- **A common toolset for every discipline:** An integrated suite serves beginners and experts.
- **Deploys anywhere:** Cloud and on-premises apps provide flexibility.

- **Single sign-on integration:** Automated license management saves you time.
- **Secure and trustworthy:** You own your content and choose how to share it.

GIS in action

This section includes real-life stories about how GIS helps support successful IT infrastructure on campus. Educational institutions are diverse, and these stories show how specific institutions successfully implement and support GIS throughout their campuses. These examples include support at Clemson University, the University of California San Diego, and Colorado State University through their respective libraries and the IT support and approach at the University of Michigan and HAS University of Applied Sciences in the Netherlands.

UNIVERSITY INSPIRES CAMPUS-WIDE GIS USE

Clemson Center for Geospatial Technologies

GROWING GLOBAL CHALLENGES, INCLUDING CLIMATE change, need creative solutions, and higher education institutions will increasingly play a vital role in empowering future generations with the knowledge, skills, tools, and interdisciplinary collaboration necessary for innovative outcomes.

One such university, Clemson University in Clemson, South Carolina, is doing so by integrating geospatial technologies within diverse academic disciplines. The Clemson Center for Geospatial Technologies (CCGT), established in 2016, fosters a community of interdisciplinary geospatial science practitioners through the support of research, teaching, and outreach activities. CCGT helps students, faculty, and researchers use GIS technology within their disciplines and create global connections between academic, industrial, governmental, and nongovernmental organizations.

Centrally located in the Cooper Library, CCGT hosts more than 3,000 people a year and teaches 11 workshops per semester to provide a basic understanding of GIS.

In addition, it serves as a resource when geospatial services are needed, including offering drone imagery, mapping, and analytics services university-wide. Participating departments have included Agriculture, Automobile Engineering, Athletics, and Campus Operations.

"This model has been a game changer in terms of collaboration to eliminate data redundancy and lower costs," said Patricia Carbajales-Dale, executive director of CCGT.

In seven years, CCGT staff have used workshops, word of mouth, department collaborations, campus events, and more to scale

Patricia Carbajales-Dale, *front left*, with her CCGT staff and interns. The center provides professional experience for interns who have gone on to work at organizations such as Amazon, Harvard University, Esri, and more.

the center to a valuable academic and operational resource. Currently, the center employs six staff members and offers internship roles. The center also facilitates workshops led by student collaborators and members from IT.

"We have a great relationship with our students and faculty, and for me, that is where our support starts. [CCGT] is a service, and our job is to support people at Clemson," said Carbajales-Dale.

IT and librarians partner to start center for geospatial technologies

The journey to create CCGT began in 2014 as a collaboration between the IT department and librarians at Clemson Library to ensure that GIS more widely benefited the campus. At the time, the university had an enterprise license agreement and seven labs dedicated to geospatial equipment. Departments such as Environmental Engineering, Forestry, and Geology were primarily the ones benefiting from GIS.

"Clemson University had a lot of investments in GIS, remote sensing, exclusive labs, but no one to directly support it. The technology was falling into the hands of faculty who were very overwhelmed," said Carbajales-Dale. "The chief information officer at the time had this vision to add a human component to the investment to make the most of the technology for the community."

That human component was Carbajales-Dale, hired in 2014 as a facilitator to ensure the impact of the technologies grew campus-wide. To expand this vision, Carbajales-Dale first offered basic GIS workshops on campus for students and faculty. The courses had high attendance rates and offered opportunities for Carbajales-Dale to learn where GIS support could enhance campus learning.

"Some departments didn't have faculty but wanted a semester-long course taught. Some faculty needed support to stay up-to-date on the technology, while students needed help with a thesis or for undergraduate research," continued Carbajales-Dale. "Our solution needed to offer flexible support; we needed to show some sort of sustainability—so we created the center."

Getting buy-in took time and a tailored approach

CCGT received funding for three years with the intent to become self-sufficient through cost-sharing of equipment, licenses, drone insurance, and so on. CCGT staff began building a sustainable foundation by nurturing buy-in from various faculty members, students, and other departments to find collaborative opportunities that met the needs of the university.

"Buy-in doesn't happen overnight. It took a few years, but we started with faculty, and we showed them by doing the things they needed that we were there to support them; they're our biggest champions," said Carbajales-Dale.

Carbajales-Dale said center staff overcame buy-in challenges by

As part of staff development efforts, Esri employees provided training to CCGT staff on machine learning and geospatial data science.

tailoring their approach to understand the users' end needs. Often this meant meeting with department chairs, lecturers, or students one-on-one to understand what technology they could benefit from in their disciplines, or even developing sample syllabi.

By 2017, the center's popularity had grown, and staff introduced a cost-sharing model through strategic partnerships with other departments. This new model moved the center toward self-sustainability while empowering staff to maintain specialized equipment and develop new support programs for remotely piloted aerial vehicles, such as drones, and lidar. By having the center and departments share costs, geospatial and imagery requests can be fulfilled within the university instead of being outsourced.

Most recently, the center and several other university departments contributed to the costs of a drone imagery project spanning the entire campus. Over 12 days, more than 7,000 high-resolution aerial photos were captured. The detailed aerial view of the campus allows departments such as Facilities to see where maintenance

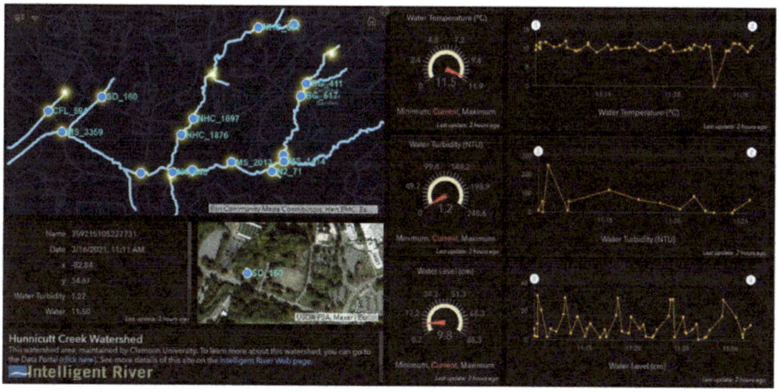

CCGT staff plan to support 40 researchers and scientists in the Intelligent River project with ArcGIS technologies to visualize and monitor the real-time data collected.

is needed. Moreover, CCGT staff used Clemson's Palmetto Cluster supercomputer to process the images and generate GIS products, such as orthomosaics and digital surface models.

"This partnership between two very centralized units, the libraries and IT, I believe, has given the center the best of both worlds," added Carbajales-Dale.

Clemson University is a land grant institution, meaning that, in addition to the work CCGT provides across campus, staff provide public services and research across the state. For example, Clemson University was awarded $3 million by the National Science Foundation (NSF) Major Research Instrumentation (MRI) program to support the Intelligent River project. The project entails designing, developing, and deploying a basin-wide network of computerized sensors to monitor water quality across the 312-mile Savannah River. CCGT staff will be using ArcGIS to help the 40 scientists on the project visualize and monitor the real-time data collected from the sensors.

Enhancing GIS curriculum through coteaching and centralized resources

Today, CCGT provides a range of services to faculty, students, administrators, and campus operations. These services include GIS fundamentals; course development; weekly workshops; outreach activities; field data collection; and access to drones, 3D printers, and lidar.

From the classroom perspective, CCGT supports six to eight classes a semester by providing workshops, lectures, or training related to the subject matter in a coteaching setup with the faculty member. Disciplines such as architecture, forestry, geology, and natural resources regularly incorporate CCGT as a resource. As part of ongoing efforts to make GIS more accessible to students in disciplines outside technology and science, staff have offered curriculum support, consultations, and training sessions for social sciences and humanities programs. These efforts have led departments such as Anthropology, Sociology, History, and Public Health to bring GIS into the classroom.

"We are beyond proud for making GIS approachable and less intimidating to all disciplines across our campus," said Elham Masoomkhah, former GIS manager at Clemson University. "Through CCGT support efforts, we have developed our GIS community from the ground up. We are humbled by an enormously increased demand for our services and are doing our best to answer the needs of our GIS community."

One example of CCGT's outreach to other disciplines is a course cotaught by Carbajales-Dale and Natallia Sianko, assistant professor in the Department of Sociology, Anthropology, and Criminal Justice at Clemson University. The class, Globalization and Social Change: Intro to GIS for Public Health, Visualization for the Social Sciences, was an interdisciplinary approach to teach students theory and technical application. The purpose of GIS in this course was to show students how to use ArcGIS StoryMaps as a tool to develop their final project. During the technical session, students set up their accounts and created a practice map.

"Social science students typically have a solid theoretical understanding of how the world works or should work, and 'hard science' majors often have a very focused view of how a specific process works. It can be difficult to pair up these two perspectives," said Sianko. "The collaboration is a perfect example of connecting the course content with technology to address challenges."

Sianko and Carbajales-Dale have collaborated multiple times on research and course content development for graduate students. In one instance, the pair worked together on a session that was part of a five-week module class. Carbajales-Dale taught a session introducing social science graduate students to graphical exploration and presentation of quantitative and qualitative data. Carbajales-Dale hopes to continue offering GIS in non-STEM courses with a future goal to extend services to the school of business.

CCGT received recognition from Esri as an official development center in 2019 and has made a lasting impact on Clemson University. To meet expanding GIS needs, the center established a GeoAmbassador program, in which postdoctoral researchers who have experience with GIS or spatial skills show undergraduates how to create a workshop to teach their peers. The center also sponsors a student-led group called the Clemson Mappers, which promotes spatial thinking and GIS on campus. Despite the pandemic, CCGT had more than 1,388 students, faculty, and staff attend its workshop series in 2020 and hit a new attendance record for the first workshop of the series.

As the world grapples with complex challenges from COVID-19 to climate change and population growth, higher education institutions will continue to find creative ways to empower students to

CCGT offers students professional development opportunities; here an intern teaches high school students field data collection in the GIS collaborative space. This intern is now a technical writer and editor with NASA Applied Sciences.

be future leaders and problem solvers. Many will follow the lead of Clemson University, imparting knowledge, skills, and the use of technology tools such as GIS. This trend toward interdisciplinary collaboration bodes well for a future in which experts across industries and nations can work together on critical issues.

A version of this story originally appeared as "Clemson Center for Geospatial Technologies Inspires Campus-Wide GIS Use" on esri.com in 2020.

UNIVERSITY MAKES GIS ACCESSIBLE ACROSS CAMPUS

University of California San Diego

STUDENTS ACROSS FIELDS AS DIVERSE AS BUSINESS, DATA science, oceanography, and urban planning are accelerating their GIS adoption with the help of synergy between Geisel Library and the Information Technology Services (ITS) department at the University of California San Diego (UCSD). Amy Work, GIS librarian, collaborated with Michael Stuart, library IT operations manager, and Maryam Sarkhoush, ITS information system analyst, to streamline access to ArcGIS through a single sign-on (SSO) experience.

So far, SSO has resulted in a dramatic increase in ArcGIS use by students, faculty, and staff. Known as enterprise login, SSO provides a seamless way to authenticate users based on their university ID, which is also used to access email, computer labs, and other resources. This integrated login experience benefits both users and administrators by reducing the number of usernames that must be remembered and managed.

Since UCSD started using SSO, the adoption rate of the ArcGIS suite of software has grown exponentially throughout the university, giving students the technology and skills to thrive academically. Ongoing collaboration between the library and ITS department is key to meeting increased demand by students, researchers, and faculty members for GIS technology access and support.

The challenge

The previous manual workflow of registering student users resulted in a low adoption rate, especially for the Web GIS technology delivered by ArcGIS Online and ArcGIS Pro. This posed a major challenge and affected students, who will need the geospatial skills gained from using the latest ArcGIS technology as they enter the workforce.

"Before SSO, we were adding new users manually to ArcGIS Online. It was a tedious job, taking our time from other productive tasks such as helping students and researchers with GIS workflows, issues with data, or discovering new approaches," said Work.

The solution

UCSD implemented enterprise login, or single sign-on (SSO), by linking its ArcGIS Online system with the university's Active Directory (AD) system. Now, across the campus community, people can use their AD accounts to get access to ArcGIS technology. In the first three months after SSO was enabled, the number of users grew from 300 to 1,000. In the following academic quarter, the number of ArcGIS users rose to 1,230, and the upward trend continues.

The key factor to successfully enabling SSO was the supportive partnership between the UCSD library and campus ITS. Whereas ITS handles back-end license and access components, the library staff has more time to support users by troubleshooting technical issues on the front end.

"The ability to collaboratively work and communicate with campus ITS has been the key factor to success because we are now able to divide and conquer incoming requests from our users," Work said.

The results

The most dramatic result of enabling SSO was the exponential increase in adoption of ArcGIS by students and faculty members from various departments, some new to GIS technology. Notable examples include ArcGIS Pro users in oceanography, ArcGIS Enterprise implementation by the Healthy Strategy Office, adoption of ArcGIS Notebooks in data science courses, and use of ArcGIS

The Data & GIS Lab in Geisel Library, UCSD.

Business Analyst™ by the Rady School of Management. Many other departments are using a variety of maps and apps, including ArcGIS StoryMaps for student projects and ArcGIS Survey123 and Quick-Capture for field data collection.

With the growing number of users, the UCSD library supports a much larger GIS community and continues to be a GIS resource center. Students can work in the Data & GIS Lab, receive support for technical questions, and attend workshops and training sessions. The library extends outreach to educators by proactively communicating through email updates, classroom visits, and periodic geospatial user meetings.

"The library is that centralized place that is discipline agnostic that anyone can come to and seek services like geospatial support," Work said.

The collaborative teams at UCSD plan on continuing the positive impact of campus-wide GIS. They are monitoring the usage and growth of GIS with a dashboard that displays which departments are users, based on enterprise logins. This approach helps the university by demonstrating the return on investment in GIS technology, which can lead to more funding for the library's GIS activities. It also helps the team understand user needs to plan future services for the campus community.

A version of this story originally appeared as "UC San Diego Makes GIS Accessible across Campus" on esri.com in 2020.

MAPPING WITHOUT BOUNDARIES: GIS REACHES ACROSS UNIVERSITY AND BEYOND

Colorado State University

INSIDE COLORADO STATE UNIVERSITY'S MORGAN LIBRARY resides the Geospatial Centroid—a GIS resource, education, and service center for students, faculty, and the greater community. Since its inception in 2009, the Centroid has grown into an invaluable resource that reaches across traditional boundaries to provide geospatial support services, hands-on training, and student internship opportunities. The culture and spirit of the Centroid welcome anyone who has the curiosity and willingness to engage.

From humble beginnings with limited financial and administrative support, the Centroid is now well established and flourishing, thanks to creative approaches, dedicated individuals, and an unwavering belief in the power of geospatial technologies to impact research, education, and action.

"The increasing importance of geospatial applications in our everyday life, economy, science, and society means that the Centroid provides an important role in providing leadership and guidance," said Dr. Melinda Laituri, former director of the Geospatial Centroid. "With its neutral position in the library, the Centroid enjoys the ability to serve any professor, researcher, or student, regardless of discipline or subject area. Spatial technologies are powerful, and the insight they can provide needs to be open and accessible to all."

Getting started

In 2009, faculty in the Warner College of Natural Resources (WCNR) initiated the concept of a center that could provide geospatial data and technical support to the campus community, focusing on common technologies and data regardless of content specialization. Originally housed within the college, the Centroid slowly built its reputation based on delivery, reliability, and consistency. One by one, GIS projects flowed in. One by one, student interns offered to volunteer to gain more professional experience.

"We started small and allowed the Centroid's services, technologies, and results to speak for themselves," noted Sophia Linn, associate director. "It was not a hard sell because the maps and GIS products proved their own worth. We simply provided a means to get there."

Getting buy-in

Soon, researchers were sharing stories about their experiences with the Centroid and their appreciation of its services. This enabled the Centroid to connect with colleges across campus to demonstrate its value. "People were interested in what the Centroid was doing and wanted to learn how geospatial technologies might help them as well," said Linn.

One of the inventive approaches the Centroid used to create cross-campus support was to occasionally offer services first. The Centroid staff would develop and present a custom-made interactive map or generate preliminary spatial data before researchers committed to a project. This provided a visual, tangible demonstration of the value of GIS. From these efforts, the Centroid was then incorporated into multiple research project proposals, leading to an increase in financial and cross-disciplinary support.

Finding a home

After five years in WCNR, the Centroid needed a new home. With strong support from the dean of libraries, who at that time also

Nelson Mwangi from Save the Elephants, *back left corner*, presents a Spatial Stories Seminar at CSU on using GPS tracking technology for elephants in Kenya.

served as the campus IT director, the Centroid moved to the library, where it received tangible resources in terms of office space, new computers, and administrative support, as well as intangible support through recognition that it now truly served the greater community.

In 2019, the Centroid was recognized as an emerging core facility by the office of the CSU vice president for research. This has been a significant boon, both financially and administratively, for the Centroid's further development and expansion.

"By design and from the start, we wanted to be certain we were building a strong foundation. Now those efforts have paid off because we had overwhelming support from all corners of campus, indicating that we truly are a core facility that supports the entire campus," said Laituri.

Outreach and education

Supporters of the Centroid continue to build awareness and offer educational opportunities. Each semester, the Centroid hosts timely

GIS training and workshops, responsive to changing technologies and the needs of the community.

Guided by Elizabeth Tulanowski, education coordinator and former Esri instructor, the Centroid also offers information about geospatial courses and geospatial help desk services. The Centroid is home to the annual GIS Day event and launched the Colorado GIS in Higher Education Summit, which is in its 10th year and held by a different Colorado institution every year. The event welcomes GIS educators to share best practices and learn from each other.

CSU is primarily an Esri shop and strives to keep current with the ever-evolving technologies. It promotes the use of ArcGIS Online as a teaching tool, supporting an increasing number of courses in using ArcGIS StoryMaps and other online tools.

CSU also manages the ArcGIS license for higher education entities throughout Colorado and works with other institutions to keep current. In addition, the Centroid recognizes the fast-paced nature of geospatial technologies and seeks to integrate ArcGIS with other open source tools.

Internship program

Anchored by a vibrant internship program, the Centroid enables motivated GIS students from any discipline to further develop their technical skills while interacting with and learning from the Centroid's diverse partners. A unique workplace on campus, the Centroid offers interns a supportive, creative, and welcoming environment.

"One of the most rewarding aspects of the Centroid is watching our student interns develop personally and professionally—from tentatively taking on new tasks to slowly embracing new challenges to then fully completing their own projects," said Linn. "The Centroid provides them with a stepping-stone between their academic learning and their future career paths beyond the university."

Students from public health, history, natural resources, and business have all passed through the Centroid. Some postgraduates have parlayed their internship experience into meaningful work. After graduating, many say that their experiences at the Centroid—specifically, their skills in GIS and real project work—gave them an advantage in landing a job or pursuing further studies.

Successes

While at the Centroid, intern Max Cook eagerly embraced any opportunity that came his way. He learned about cartography, Python programming, model building, web mapping development, and remote sensing while also serving as a go-to person for problem solving and help desk assistance. In addition, Cook contributed to a project for The Nature Conservancy (TNC). Upon graduation, he was hired by TNC, for his experience, attitude, and value to the organization. Cook is now in graduate school in geography and geospatial science, while still maintaining a part-time position with TNC.

Another intern, Brandon Lemire, also fully engaged with his internship experience. Highly skilled technically, Lemire contributed to the technical infrastructure of the Centroid as a student. He also gained a diversity of new skills while working on projects for the National Park Service (NPS), among others. Upon graduation, Lemire was hired by NPS as its remote sensing lead.

Jamie Hoover, the first intern employed by the Centroid, worked on multiple projects, including developing an application to analyze wind data and planning the first GIS in Higher Education Summit. She has since completed her PhD and now is a full-time instructor in GIS and remote sensing at Front Range Community College.

While CSU's Geospatial Centroid fills a need for the Fort Collins campus and community, it also provides an example for other organizations wanting to establish cross-disciplinary GIS services.

Institutions interested in establishing a similar center are encouraged to reach out to Geospatial Centroid staff to learn more.

A version of this story originally appeared as "Mapping without Boundaries: Geospatial Centroid Reaches across University and Beyond" on esri.com in 2020.

SCALING UP GIS ACROSS CAMPUS

University of Michigan

AT THE UNIVERSITY OF MICHIGAN, GIS ISN'T STORED AWAY in a technology department or restricted to science or technology majors. "It takes more effort to restrict access to specific units than to make GIS available to everyone," said Peter Knoop, research computing consultant at the University of Michigan. Although he is based in the College of Literature, Science, and the Arts (LSA), Knoop has enabled autoprovisioned enterprise logins for faculty, staff, and students across the university. The result is an enterprise-class, scalable, and robust GIS environment in which independent, dispersed support staff assist with the use of GIS and facilitate its adoption in nontraditional domains, rather than spending time managing access to GIS resources.

Clean Wolverines together on campus

The class EARTH 380—"Mineral Resources, Economics, and the Environment"—focuses on effective scientific communication, fulfilling an upper-level writing requirement for undergraduate students. It includes a semester-long project exploring alternative energy options for the university's electricity supply. The project serves as the context in which students develop their communication skills and use ArcGIS GeoPlanner℠ and ArcGIS StoryMaps for several assignments. In 2017, a group of students was motivated to further explore the topic, forming the Clean Wolverines, who eventually hosted a campus meeting, Toward Carbon Neutrality at the University of Michigan: 2025 and Beyond. The group remains active, attracting new students from within and outside the course each year, and their ongoing efforts helped prompt a university presidential initiative to pursue carbon neutrality.

Enhancing digital humanities courses with ArcGIS StoryMaps

The use of ArcGIS StoryMaps stories has become a mainstay in many humanities courses (Judaic studies, anthropology, history, and English, to name a few) at the University of Michigan. Shachar Pinsker, professor of Judaic studies, worked with Knoop on ArcGIS StoryMaps assignments that help students understand the spatial relations of cafés and their key roles as centers of political, financial, scientific, and literary exchange in the late 19th and early 20th centuries. Working with a team including Knoop, Pinsker recently released an app that is a mashup of ArcGIS StoryMaps, ArcGIS API for JavaScript, and Scalar. The app serves as a stand-alone site for exploring this topic and as a digital companion for Pinsker's book *A Rich Brew: How Cafés Created Modern Jewish Culture* (NYU Press, 2018).

Innovation pathways—GIS in on-site work

By testing new technology with a small group of motivated and fault-tolerant collaborators, Knoop has found a way to test GIS technology and develop best practices to speed and ease adoption by the broader university community. This is the case for Collector, Survey123, and ArcGIS Explorer. By accompanying the collaborators in their work and providing on-site GIS and IT support, he enables them to safely try out new approaches, identifying what works (and what doesn't). In turn, this allows Knoop and his team to train other groups to use these tools on their own. Over time, the willingness of members of the Kelsey Museum of Archaeology and the university's Department of Earth and Environmental Sciences (EARTH) to experiment with new approaches to GIS, for example, has yielded benefits for numerous field-based teaching and research activities across the university.

3D reconstructions done on-site using ArcGIS Pro

GIS is helping archaeologists at the University of Michigan and their collaborators integrate and explore spatial data from different sources and at varied scales. Using drone imagery, lidar, ground-penetrating radar, photogrammetry, geophysical measurements, and more, researchers are using ArcGIS to directly record data digitally and develop 3D reconstructions, enhancing understanding of their site. Examples include the Notion Archaeological Survey, revealing a well-preserved and almost completely unexplored ancient city in Türkiye; the Olynthos Project, exploring aspects of the society and economy of an ancient city in northern Greece; and the Gabii Project, studying the development and structure of Archaic urban planning in central Italy. ArcGIS assists in other ways as well—for example, aiding studies of the provenance of pottery and using geochemical analysis, geologic maps, and watershed analysis for the Olynthos Project.

A version of this story originally appeared as "Scaling Up GIS across Campus" on esri.com in 2019.

UNIVERSITY EMPOWERS CAMPUS-WIDE GIS

HAS University of Applied Sciences

LOCATED IN 'S-HERTOGENBOSCH, A CITY IN THE Netherlands, HAS University of Applied Sciences is an independent institution specializing in agriculture, food, the environment, horticulture, and nature studies. With more than 3,000 degree-seeking and professional students, HAS University consistently ranks as a top midsize university for applied sciences in the Netherlands because of its mission to provide real-life experiences for students and promote lifelong learning. At its core, the university focuses on providing entrepreneurial study with day-to-day business practices, often having students collaborate with both local and international businesses in their coursework.

The university's Applied Geo-Information Science program continues to fulfill the institution's mission by preparing the next generation of successful geospatial experts for diverse careers. Throughout the four-year bachelor's degree program, students learn how to combine geography, media, and design into novel products and services. In 2016, program organizers saw that—with changing trends in business needs, technological advances, and the amount of data available—GIS instruction could benefit programs campus-wide. Accordingly, program leaders sought to enable campus-wide access to GIS technology.

The challenge

HAS University's IT policy requires full integration of all software used by students. Consequently, connecting student accounts to online GIS software with individualized passwords proved to be a time-consuming process for the university's IT department during setup and security maintenance. The old model also discouraged collaborative projects because students couldn't readily share data. If students and faculty outside the Applied Geo-Information Science program were to truly benefit from GIS, the technology had to be easier for the IT department to access and maintain.

The solution

HAS University implemented enterprise login, or single sign-on (SSO), by linking its ArcGIS Online system with the university's Microsoft Active Directory (AD) system. Now students and faculty across campus can use their AD accounts to access ArcGIS Online at any time and on any device they choose. With SSO, ArcGIS technology is one more application students can access along with their email, datasets, school apps, and so forth, without the need for secondary authentication.

"Before SSO, we were individually connecting students to their

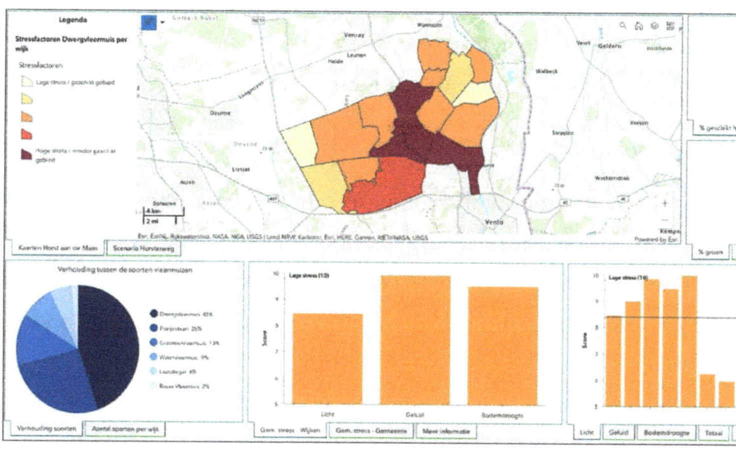

Example of a fourth-year student's final thesis dashboard, created to inform policy makers and citizens about biodiversity in the neighborhood (in this case, bats), with details including stress factors, percentage of suitable habitat, and subdivisions of stress (light, noise, and dryness of soil).

accounts and the ArcGIS Online environment. It cost a lot of time and was the biggest technical challenge we had in moving online a few years ago," said Koen Verschuren, then supervisor for HAS University's Applied Geo-Information Science program.

The results

Since the implementation of SSO, not only has technical assistance time from IT significantly decreased but the number of ArcGIS Online users has also grown across departments and disciplines.

"With SSO and the straightforward interface, it is much easier for students to experiment with the software—we're especially seeing more non-GIS course users using ArcGIS Online," said Marien de Bakker, senior lecturer and project manager for the Applied Geo-Information Science program.

A key factor in successfully enabling enterprise login was the collaborative relationship between HAS University of Applied Sciences—the IT department, information security staff, and the program leads—and Esri Netherlands.

"I have always really liked all the data that is available with ArcGIS and that the software operates in a way that students can easily work with it," continued de Bakker. "And I'm very happy with Esri Netherlands in how the company has changed from being a software provider for the university to a more integral solution provider."

Other positive results of enabling enterprise login included updates to the curriculum, which allowed students to achieve more with their lessons.

"The user interface is enormously easier compared to 15 years ago, and so lessons that would, say, take 80 or 120 hours to learn can now be cut down to 4 hours with ArcGIS Online," said de Bakker.

De Bakker added that there has been an immense growth in the number of students now using the software to approach real-world challenges.

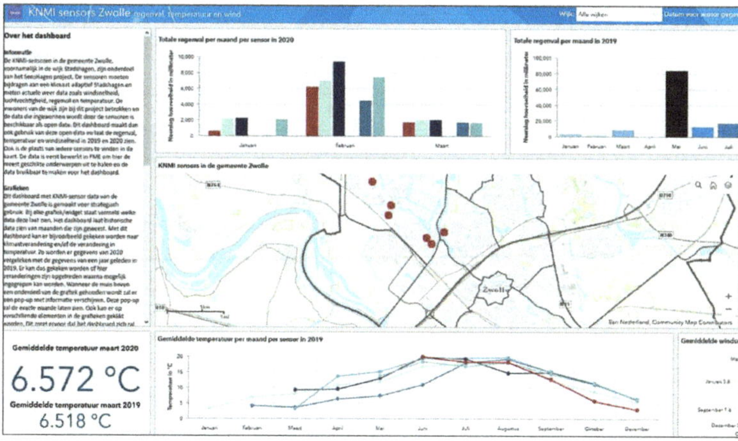

Example of a second-year student's dashboard featuring sensors of the Dutch Royal Meteorological Institute. The sensor data includes rainfall, temperature, and wind, used as an example of the smart city concept.

"We're seeing students working through harder societal and business questions using ArcGIS Online. The questions are not, 'How do I use this technology?' but instead, 'What questions and challenges can I now answer with this technology?'" he said.

With the growing number of users, de Bakker hopes to continue seeing students and faculty of diverse backgrounds embrace GIS technology for their careers. To date, students who have graduated from the Applied Geo-Information Science program have gone on to accept roles in city planning, consultancy, government, education, engineering, public safety, utilities, and real estate. De Bakker credits the program's educational material, internships, and recent SSO integration with ArcGIS Online for ensuring continued student success at HAS University.

A version of this story originally appeared as "HAS University of Applied Sciences Empowers Campus-Wide GIS" on esri.com in 2020.

PART 4

ADMINISTRATORS

GIS FOR SMART CAMPUS OPERATIONS PROVIDES INSIGHTS on how to minimize risk, maximize return on investments in facilities, and promote sustainable practices. You can drive efficiencies by using live indoor and outdoor maps to deliver real-time operational awareness of facility space, asset inventories, utilities, building conditions, and public safety. With GIS for facilities, you can easily visualize facility status information in 2D and 3D and identify poor productivity patterns.

Campus facilities

Facility managers achieve success by using powerful data management, analysis, and visualization tools. A digital approach to facility management helps leaders assess security risks, develop plans, optimize space use, protect staff and assets, and improve daily operations. GIS for facilities helps lay the cornerstone for a campus digital twin, a virtual representation of the real world, including physical objects, processes, relationships, and behaviors.

Campus utilities

GIS contains all the elements that staff members need to meet utility challenges. They can use GIS to maintain key information, analyze it, and distribute it to everyone who needs business intelligence through a system of record, a system of engagement, and a system of insights. This process creates a true digital twin of the campus infrastructure. GIS helps a campus save energy and achieve its sustainability goals.

Campus health and safety

Whether you need to know the real-time location of officers and staff on campus, analyze historical incidents of crime to understand campus risk, or generate Clery Act reports required of colleges and universities and information requests on campus crime data, GIS brings spatial analysis to the forefront of informed decision-making and enhanced campus security and safety.

GIS in action

This section looks at real-life stories about how GIS helps support school administrators. Read these stories to learn how GIS enables schools, colleges, and universities to manage multiple buildings on their campuses, promote equitable services, program litter management, consolidate facilities and amenities, manage all holdings, ensure the health of students and faculty during a pandemic, and crowdsource mapping to update utilities.

SCHOOL DISTRICT INTEGRATES CAD AND GIS FOR PLANNING

Albuquerque Public Schools

FOUNDED IN 1891, ALBUQUERQUE PUBLIC SCHOOLS (APS) in Albuquerque, New Mexico, is the 34th-largest school district in the US, serving 83,000 students. With a mission to provide comprehensive and high-quality education in partnership with school staff, families, and the local community, APS strives to prepare students for college and beyond with a challenging curriculum and supportive environment.

APS maintains 16 million square feet of built environment with district facilities and more than 140 elementary schools, middle schools, and high schools. The management of facilities and infrastructure in the school district involves a GIS for mapping and spatial analysis as well as computer-aided design (CAD) data, which allows professionals to design and document real-world objects.

CAD data was originally managed outside the GIS, posing a challenge for the APS school planning team, designers, and maintenance workers when analyzing data, planning for future buildings, and maintaining current structures. To successfully integrate CAD data into its GIS, APS enlisted Esri Professional Services to develop a new workflow to help it better manage and analyze the data.

The challenge

APS combines ArcGIS technology, CAD data, and student information systems to perform complex data analysis by spatially mapping and layering features, such as facility data points, physical amenities, and the number of students in classrooms. The results from this advanced analysis help the school planning team and school officials identify students' needs and deficiencies in the built environment.

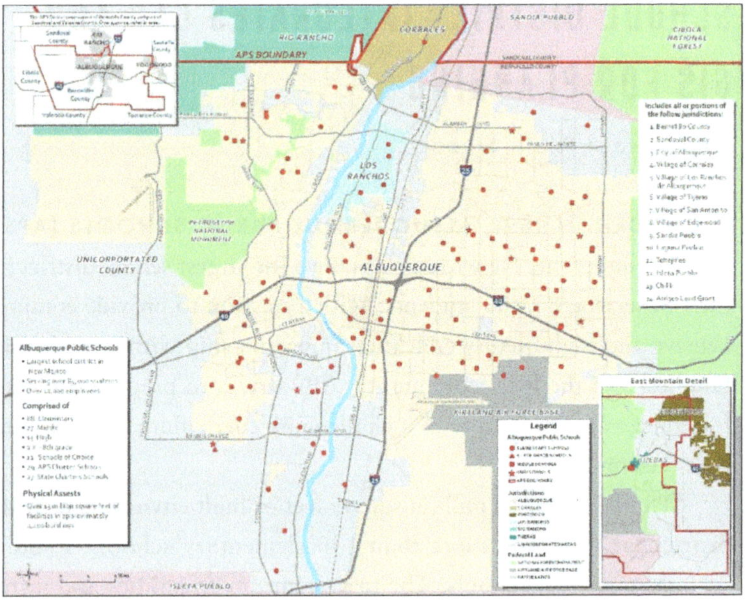

APS district map showing 14 overlapping jurisdictions, 88 elementary schools, 27 middle schools, 2 K–8 schools, and 11 schools of choice.

For many years, a considerable challenge for APS was having its large datasets managed in separate systems and divisions. This type of data analysis was time-consuming for the district's school planning team.

APS wanted a new one-stop-shop solution that allowed it to integrate existing CAD data into its GIS to help school planners with site master planning, utilization and capacity studies, and facility assessment. The solution needed to be accessible district-wide so the GIS team could perform real-time spatial analysis accurately and efficiently.

"We already do so much analysis in GIS with school boundaries and student demographics [that] we thought, why not take it to the next level and uncover the unlimited possibilities by bringing facility data into GIS?" said Elizabeth Halpin, American Institute of

Certified Planners (AICP), then senior planner and manager for the Albuquerque Public Schools Capital Master Plan.

The solution

To successfully integrate CAD data into GIS, APS needed to bring together facility and geospatial datasets that are typically used on different software platforms. In 2012, APS began the process of digitizing paper CAD drawings and now maintains standardized digital CAD drawings for 158 district facilities with 1,787 individual buildings. The interior space of these buildings includes portables and modular spaces.

With such a large dataset, APS needed to identify the optimal workflow and tools to bring CAD data into GIS. According to Halpin, ensuring the compatibility of the CAD data with GIS standards became the biggest challenge in the conversion process. The school planning team turned to Esri Professional Services to advise the CAD and GIS technical staff on the best starting point.

Grady Snipes with Esri Professional Services met with APS to develop the solution through site visits, training sessions, and meetings. Snipes advised the APS team on the best practices for working with the CAD data—running their GIS tools, setting up configuration files, and determining the entire workflow process to successfully complete the process.

According to Halpin, several phases of standardization were developed, including measuring square footage and creating building outlines. Larger CAD drawings for each campus were divided into individual drawings for each building and floor.

After the georeferencing process, Esri's Floorplan To Indoors tool was used to convert CAD drawings to GIS. A quality control process was implemented to ensure the completeness and accuracy of the data.

"Seeing that first drawing appear on-screen in GIS was a visual

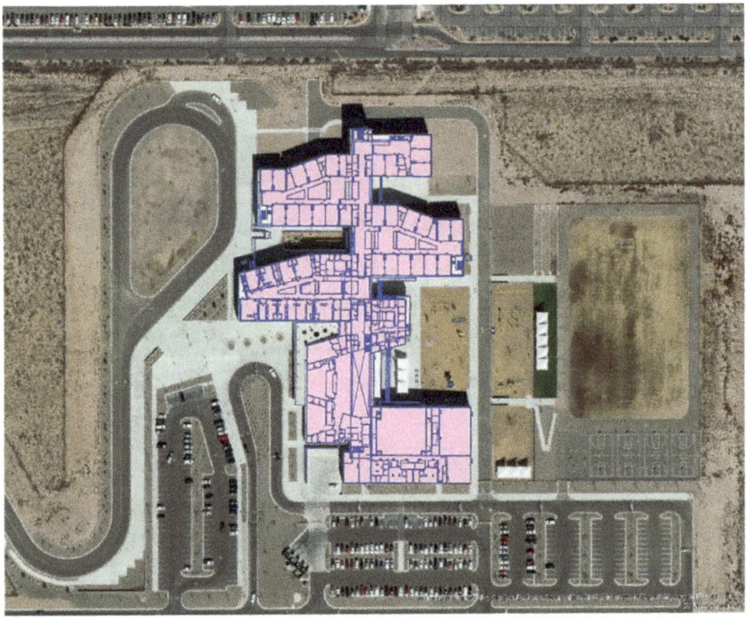

George I. Sánchez K–8 School aerial map with floor plans overlay.

success and a big moment of celebration for our team," said Tammira Taylor, GIS planner for the Albuquerque Public Schools Capital Master Plan.

The results

With the help of Esri Professional Services, APS uncovered the most efficient way to bring CAD data into GIS. Once there, a documented workflow allowed APS to troubleshoot the CAD data in GIS on its own. The team worked collaboratively to review the CAD data and perform fixes, eventually distributing the data across the district.

"Establishing a workflow enabled us to take ownership of the data and fix issues as they came along. The step-by-step workflow was essential in enabling us to dive into the details," said Taylor.

APS was invited to present this initiative at the 2019 Education Summit at the Esri User Conference in San Diego. While there, Halpin and Taylor presented the CAD integration initiative and connected with other districts that wanted to do the same. They were also invited to deliver the same presentation and workshop at GIS in the Rockies, an annual geospatial information and technology conference.

The APS school planning team planned to continue its collaboration with Esri Professional Services when it began implementing ArcGIS Indoors™ in fall 2020. Indoors is a complete interior mapping system. With this implementation, APS would be the first public school district in the United States to use this technology for smart building management.

The team wanted the same integration of CAD data into GIS for analysis of interior and exterior areas. This would allow APS to layer educational programmatic data into the facility data and do planning analyses in different areas, such as identifying appropriate spaces to integrate special education into the general education setting.

"Overall, the experience with Esri Professional Services was positive and effective," said Halpin. "I look forward to working with them on the deployment of Indoors. School facility planning and design practitioners are excited to see the results."

A version of this story originally appeared as "New Mexico School District Integrates CAD, GIS with Esri Technology and Services" on esri.com in 2020.

ONLINE SCHOOLING PROMPTS MUNICIPALITIES TO MAP DIGITAL INEQUITIES

Philadelphia and Palm Beach School Districts

AS THE CORONAVIRUS PANDEMIC ENDANGERED AND upended the lives of millions over the past couple of years, it has perhaps affected no group more universally than children. Adults fortunate enough to retain jobs they could do from home are at least familiar with the concept of remote work. For kids, live video classwork reflects an alien pedagogy, and the lack of in-person peer interaction hinders the development of social skills.

Pivoting to computer-based remote learning also deepened existing fault lines in American education. With broadband now integral to schoolwork, researchers at the Pew Research Center have documented a widening homework gap.

Teens in households earning less than $30,000 are nearly three times as likely as households with incomes above $75,000 to report having trouble completing homework assignments because of lack of access to a computer or reliable broadband connection. Nearly half of teens in low-income families say they sometimes do their homework on a cell phone.

Pew also found that the homework gap involves racial disparities. More than one in five Black teens are forced to search out public Wi-Fi sources for connectivity. Hispanic teens are twice as likely as White teens to report they lack access to a home computer.

The pandemic made the problem impossible to ignore. “The digital divide was suddenly starkly apparent,” said Mark Wheeler, director of the City of Philadelphia’s Office of Innovation and Technology

(OIT). "There were families who couldn't afford reliable internet. They were using whatever they could to get by—public computing centers, free Wi-Fi through businesses, libraries—and with those shuttered, we had a sizable population that couldn't participate in daily life."

The school closures that roiled American life at the beginning of the pandemic underscored a crisis within a crisis. Almost overnight, school districts, especially those with large populations of students from low-income families, had to devise ways to keep the gap from swallowing students whole. Here, we look at what happened in two of the largest school districts in the US.

From Philly to Florida, a common goal

At first glance, the city and county of Philadelphia would seem to have little in common with southeastern Florida's Palm Beach County. Each has a population of around 1.5 million, but Philadelphia's is squeezed into an area one-sixteenth the size of its distant neighbor on the tropical end of the Eastern Seaboard. Philadelphia has twice the poverty, two-thirds the median income, and significantly less sunshine.

Scratch the surface, however, and Philadelphia and Palm Beach look more alike. Although Philadelphia is one of America's poorest large cities, it contains pockets of high affluence. Although Palm Beach County's considerable wealth is mostly concentrated on the Atlantic coast, in cities such as Palm Beach and Boca Raton, poverty persists in several communities sandwiched between the ocean and the I-95 freeway. The poverty rate in the Glades, the inland area near Lake Okeechobee, is higher than Philadelphia's, and the median income is much lower.

Philadelphia and Palm Beach also share a civic quirk. Both counties consolidate their schools into a single school district that each serves around 200,000 students. One out of every 130 public school pupils in the country lives in one of these two districts.

The arrival of COVID-19 forced the school districts of Philadelphia and Palm Beach County to quickly determine before the school year ended who was most at risk of being left behind.

Palm Beach rises to the challenge

Each district acquired 80,000 Chromebook computers, using a combination of philanthropic and public funds. To understand better who most needed computers, and how to ensure that these students and others also had broadband access, both districts adopted similar data-driven approaches.

To assess needs, the Palm Beach County schools' Division of Performance Accountability sought the advice of Donna Goldstein, an IT manager and GIS expert with the district.

Goldstein began her analysis by using geocoded student data to see where students lived. The data contained demographic information relating to each student, which could be displayed as layers on a map showing where incomes were lowest. She could also see who had already accessed the online student portal.

Goldstein's team was especially interested in students coded as eligible for subsidized school lunches, thinking these might be families with limited access to technology. Using GIS, she performed a point density analysis that displayed geographic clusters of families, which Goldstein then color-coded into three levels of concentration.

These clusters helped the county determine where to place Wi-Fi hot spots, pole-mounted transmitters that broadcast Wi-Fi signals that students nearby can access with a special receiver.

To refine the data, Goldstein added more layers, including municipalities, census tract data, and the locations of neighborhoods already earmarked for community revitalization funds. She also mapped housing subdivisions because the county would need to request easements to install the receivers on private property.

The map also helped the county plan where to lay fiber to bring the signals to the Glades. To reach far-flung homes, officials used the map to pick buildings on which to mount poles, including schools, a church, a library, and an Animal Care and Control office.

"We combined all this data to give us a really well-rounded view of what's going on in the county, and where the greatest areas of need were," Goldstein said. "If the team wasn't able to work with the data geographically, and had to look through raw databases, I don't know how long it would've taken, but it would've been an extraordinarily long time."

Bridging the digital divide in Philadelphia

Meanwhile, a similar process was unfolding in Philadelphia. A program called PHLConnectED, a joint effort launched by OIT and the Mayor's Office of Education, was helping families obtain computers and establish home Wi-Fi hot spots while also making plans to establish community computing access centers. By late October 2020, more than 11,000 public school families were receiving free internet access, thanks to the collaborative efforts of city government, the school district, and business and philanthropic leaders.

As in Palm Beach, the initial difficulty PHLConnectED faced was how to identify families that needed the program the most. Those experiencing housing insecurity were hard to contact. An even bigger problem was finding families in relatively stable situations but with limited incomes. "We have to make them realize what we offer them is free, and that this isn't a rug that will be pulled out from under them after a few weeks," Wheeler said.

To help organize efforts, Wheeler's office tapped CityGeo, a dedicated team within OIT devoted to mapping and spatial analysis.

CityGeo was already using GIS to maintain a city stress index that compiles geographic data on crime, homelessness, drug abuse, and other issues that might suggest the existence of students in need. The data helped PHLConnectED prioritize the distribution of wireless routers to create mobile hot spots for students.

"A lot of our work is focused not only on mapping, but on keeping data dynamically up-to-date through the dashboard," said Hank Garie, CityGeo's then geographic information officer. "So, whether it's meal sites or access centers, it's all fed into the GIS, which gives us a great way to visualize and analyze where we might want to target outreach programs based on need or affordability."

Post-COVID, closing the larger gap

The progress made around bridging the homework gap in Philadelphia and Palm Beach County has implications for broader equity issues. "As spinoffs from this initiative, we've been able to do parallel work with our Commerce Department," Garie said. "A lot of these same datasets are applicable, and we can even use them to view the city's budget through an equity lens."

Wheeler noted frequent references to the stress index in city meetings because, he said, the spatial analysis "really brings into stark relief that so much of this is about where people live."

"The work the CityGeo team has done has really laid the groundwork for me, as a CIO (chief information officer), to have conversations at the mayor's level about where populations we're trying to reach live and how they're aligned with so many other critical problems we're trying to solve in the pandemic," Wheeler said.

Goldstein agreed. "For me, it goes beyond kids," she said. "That's our primary focus, but now you've got parents and other adults in the home who have broadband access, which opens up whole new worlds of possibilities for them economically."

She sees the effort as providing a small silver lining during the crisis. “From my perspective, this is one of the only good things to come out of the pandemic,” she added. “As educators, we’ve been fighting the digital divide for eons. So this is really exciting.”

A version of this story by Patricia Cummens originally appeared as "Online Schooling Prompts Municipalities to Map Digital Inequities" on the Esri Blog on November 12, 2020.

UNIVERSITY USES GIS TO RETHINK CAMPUS LITTER MANAGEMENT

Michigan State University

REALIZING THAT MAINTENANCE WORKERS WERE WASTING their time servicing trash receptacles that were rarely or never used around campus, Adam Lawver, the campus services director at Michigan State University (MSU), looked to GIS to help solve the problem.

To save the workers time and lower the annual cost of maintaining more than 400 waste bins, the staff decided to eliminate those receptacles that were rarely being used.

But where were these often-empty bins located on the sprawling, 2,000-acre campus in East Lansing? Which ones were no longer needed? Could more efficient routes be created for maintenance workers emptying and cleaning the most used trash cans, saving time and labor costs?

For the answers, Lawver's team sought a technology-based solution using location-based data. Lawver contacted Jade Freeman, GIS coordinator for the spatial data management team in the MSU IT Analytics and Data Solutions department, who used ArcGIS technology to guide landscape services staff to collect data on the bins and analyze which bins were underutilized.

First, a geodatabase was designed to capture information about the types of bins on campus, their locations, and related maintenance and service records. The services were published in ArcGIS Enterprise. Then, a map was created in ArcGIS Online that highlighted bins that needed service based on their service frequency and last service data. Workers used ArcGIS Collector to map each bin location and gather maintenance data each time they serviced one of the 436 bins on campus, providing the information needed to decide—after

The Litter Operations Dashboard shows key metrics, such as the number of trash receptacles that need to be serviced at any given time.

a 90-day trial period—which receptacles were rarely used and could be removed.

"We wanted to reduce the number of containers campus-wide based on measuring utilization through GIS technology," Lawver said.

Lawver and Freeman led this project to transform litter management on campus, a process that had stayed relatively unchanged for decades.

"We were able to quickly design a solution that allowed bins to be mapped to keep track of frequency patterns," Freeman said. "That really illustrated the power of what GIS could do."

Lawver and Freeman planned and worked together to integrate GIS technology into the litter management system at MSU and streamline the process through the following:

- Reducing labor and equipment costs by 50 percent, resulting in a cost savings of $215,000 annually by the fourth year of implementation

- Engaging frontline and office staff to use GIS software, including Collector and ArcGIS Dashboards
- Reallocating hours to perform other core maintenance tasks
- Partnering with MSU's College of Engineering to further improve the program

Hurdles to overcome

MSU began to use GIS technology to completely transform litter management for its campus in 2014. However, the initiative faced several challenges, including the following:

- No known data or records of the number of receptacles on campus were available.
- No records existed of the most efficient routes to take to service all the receptacles.
- Too much time was being spent servicing rarely used bins, resulting in time away from other core maintenance tasks.
- Employees performed litter management based on intuition and experience, but passing along this knowledge to new employees was sometimes difficult.

Historically, litter management processes were shared when new employees were onboarded. This transfer of knowledge from employee to employee resulted in a process based mainly on habits and intuition rather than the establishment of a defined route for servicing the bins.

"Employees would drive around to each trash can in the 180 acres they were responsible for," Lawver said. "None of them were provided with the most efficient route in their area, nor was there information to tell them which bins needed service."

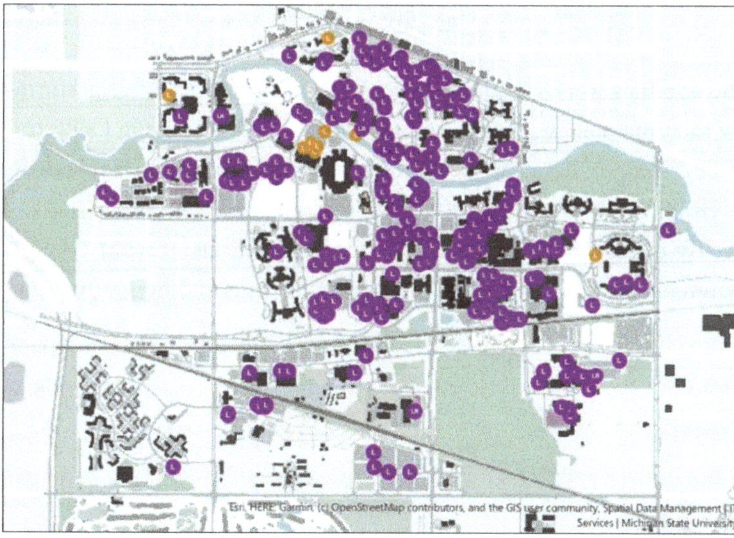

This is the map that workers open in ArcGIS Collector. It shows the receptacles that need to be emptied per their service frequency setting and last service date.

MSU mobilizes the workforce

After the location data on the trash bins was collected and mapped, it was published as feature classes so that attributes could be assigned. During the mapping process, the landscape services team learned there were 436 bins on the MSU property.

Employees then used Collector on Apple iPads or iPhones to update the status and appropriate service interval for the receptacles. Each time a bin was emptied, it was entered as a related record in Collector, and the service interval was adjusted as needed (e.g., weekly, biweekly, or monthly).

Employees also used the app to note whether the receptacle needed repairs or whether the container should be moved to another area on campus.

Uncovering patterns with GIS

The 436 bins were set up on a weekly service rotation. After performing their maintenance tasks, employees recorded the data in Collector. After collecting data for six months, the team deployed Dashboards to visualize the information.

By using that dashboard to study the patterns of what type of maintenance was being done on each of the bins and how often, the

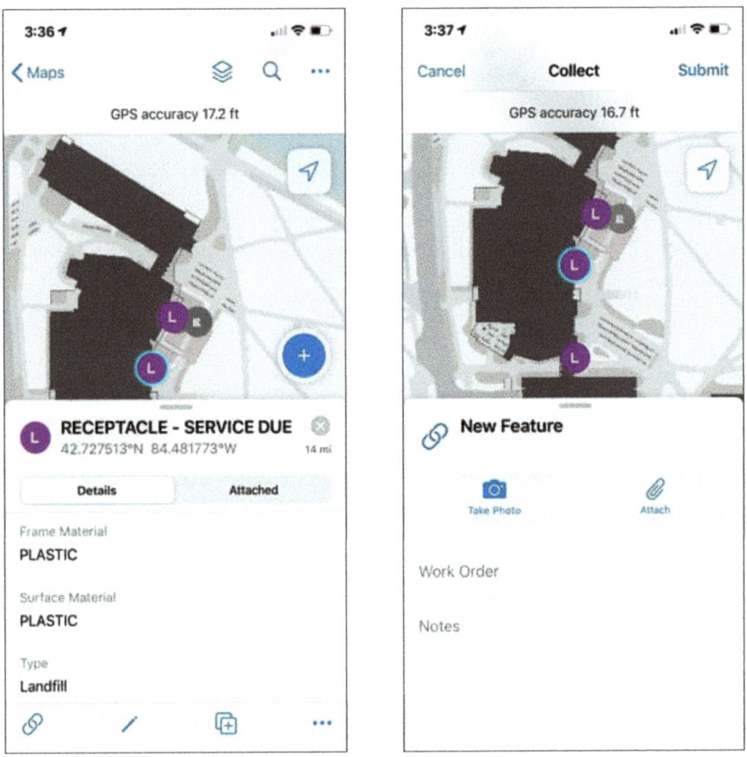

In Collector, workers can see information about an individual trash receptacle (*left*). From this screen, the user can edit the details or add service and maintenance records. Workers can use the Collector app to note the location and other details about a new litter receptacle (*right*).

leadership team found that 200 bins needed servicing only once every two months. Eventually, those trash receptacles were eliminated completely in favor of ones used more regularly.

Implementing Dashboards also gave employees a way to see the progress they were making toward monthly and yearly goals. This built trust among teams, increased morale, fostered mutual respect between workers and supervisors, and inspired pride and accountability.

Cutting litter management costs in half

The most significant result of the project was the drop in litter management costs.

Labor and equipment costs in 2015 were $445,000, and in 2018 that figure dropped to $230,000, a 50 percent decrease in labor and equipment costs for litter management.

The hours spent servicing the trash bins can now be allocated toward performing more productive maintenance tasks, giving employees the opportunity to increase their skill sets in other areas.

MSU has now become highly efficient at using ArcGIS to better manage litter. The number of employees working on litter management has dropped from 40 employees to one full-time worker and a student assistant.

Bin capacity sensor becomes student capstone project

Other opportunities remain to further refine the litter management routes and inform employees when to service bins.

In 2018, the College of Engineering Design Day program started collaborating with Kris Jolley from MSU's Surplus Store and Recycling center to have MSU students design and build a capacity sensor for receptacles as a capstone project.

"Bin capacity sensor technology informs staff when to service

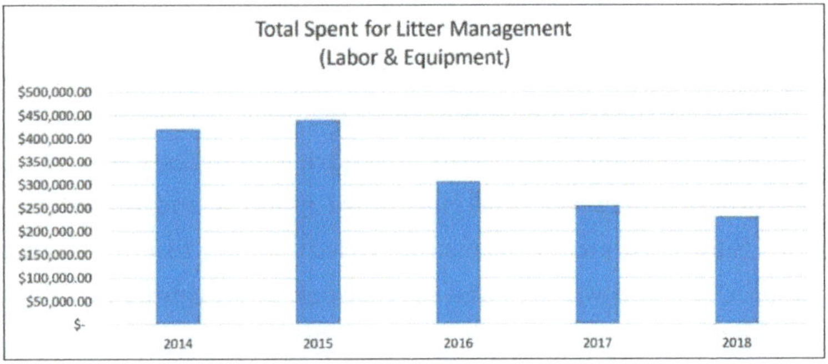

The total cost spent on litter management decreased significantly from 2014 to 2018—and by 50 percent from 2015 to 2018.

receptacles, eliminating wasteful trips [and] reducing trash overflow," Lawver said.

The student team built a sensor prototype, but as testing on the prototype began, team members identified alternative commercially available capacity sensors. These sensors have the potential to integrate with GIS software and alert employees on their mobile devices when a receptable is at 75 percent capacity and requires service. Students were still able to learn from their work developing the project.

What's next: Automating litter management through GIS and network patterns

Lawver and his team will continue to build on the idea of sensor technology integration with bins using GIS across campus. In fall 2019, bin servicing shifted to the Surplus and Recycling department, resulting in further savings in labor and equipment costs. Now, GIS offers the potential for other initiatives such as deploying mobile robotics for automating litter management.

In the future, GIS may be used to create a network of patterns of when receptacles need to be serviced. That pattern of code can trigger mobile robots to navigate to the bins requiring service and empty them, returning the debris to a larger bin. The larger bin would then be serviced by a trash truck.

"One way or another, new technologies will shape how and what we do," Lawver said. "The critical question is how we, as leaders, build trust to foster a workplace that inspires high performance and flexibility in response to emerging technologies."

A version of this story by Rosemary Boone originally appeared as "A Thrifty Idea: Michigan State University Uses GIS to Rethink and Innovate Litter Management on Campus" in the October 2020 issue of *ArcWatch*.

NEW UNIVERSITY CAMPUS INCORPORATES GIS FROM THE OUTSET

Sabah Al-Salem University City—Kuwait University

SABAH AL-SALEM UNIVERSITY CITY, WHICH WILL SOON contain all the buildings and colleges associated with Kuwait University, is "one of the largest educational campuses in the world," according to its website. Known as Sabah Al-Salem University City—Kuwait University, or SSUC-KU, the campus is one of Kuwait's main development projects. GIS has been the backbone of SSUC-KU's project life cycle since the beginning and will continue to shape day-to-day activities at the university for years to come.

Managing all data and assets with GIS

Previously, Kuwait University's colleges were scattered in different locations throughout the country. Traffic around those campuses was severe, and the buildings couldn't absorb the growing number of students.

The new, consolidated SSUC-KU campus has all the facilities and amenities needed to offer a modern education. In all, SSUC-KU's two campuses span 2.3 square miles and are designed to accommodate 40,000 students. The main campus, which contains the university's 11 humanities and science colleges and covers 1.5 square miles, consists of 22 buildings. The health sciences campus, which is still being designed, will fill 0.75 square miles and host the university's 5 medical colleges in about 25 buildings.

The intention is to manage all SSUC-KU assets and data—whether spatial or nonspatial—using GIS. To achieve that, the campus's master plan was developed alongside the first version of its GIS data model, using a combination of industry-specific GIS data models

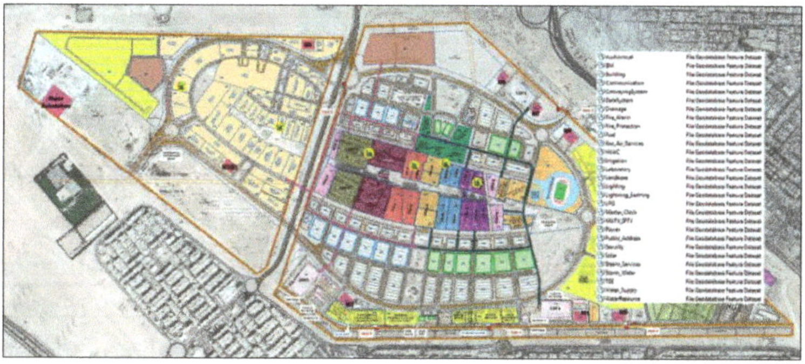

The master plan for SSUC-KU was developed in conjunction with the university's GIS data model.

covering all expected services, including water, electricity, and telecommunications. As the construction process got under way, the data model needed to be extended to absorb new datasets, feature classes, domains, and subtypes. The latest version of the data model contains 29 datasets, 433 feature classes, 58 geodatabase tables, and 21 relationship classes.

As some of the colleges on the main campus were getting ready to receive students in September 2019, the team at Openware, Esri's official distributor in Kuwait and the GIS consultant on the project, used ArcMap and ArcGIS Pro to ensure a smooth transition from the old university to the new campus. In fact, GIS became the primary tool used for decision-making. Staff in various departments requested hundreds of reports to help them locate their spaces and services on maps. For example, employees in the Department of Libraries requested maps showing all the library facilities in each building so they could arrange their supplies and revamp their workflows. Staff in the Services Department, meanwhile, requested maps showing all the electrical rooms, telecommunications pathways and spaces, and other assets throughout the campus so they could situate their teams appropriately.

A portal, some apps, and a dashboard

Once the campuses are in full service, university staff, faculty, students, and visitors will need to be able to find various buildings and rooms and figure out where to go on the new campus. In that regard, Openware developed a bilingual—Arabic and English—mobile portal that contains search apps. The locate subsystem within the portal is built on Elasticsearch technology and uses the ArcGIS Indoors Information Model, which draws a route for each search result based on the user's current location. The portal also includes outdoor mapping functionality, which contains a map that shows the campus's street network and basic outdoor infrastructure, taken from the SSUC-KU master plan. The map can even be extended beyond the campus—and throughout the entire state of Kuwait—to make navigation to and from the area seamless.

The mobile portal contains various apps as well. One app allows inspectors with special privileges to generate work orders and assign tasks to field maintenance crews. The app consumes Archibus

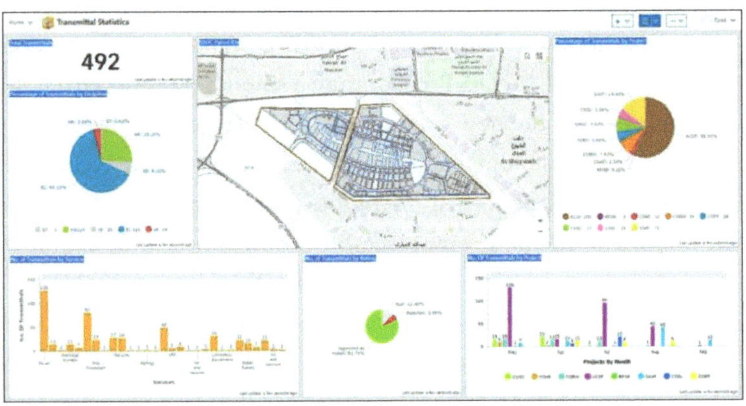

Openware uses ArcGIS Dashboards to show the flow of data through GIS at SSUC-KU, broken down by month, discipline, project, and business.

database tables inside Survey123 forms, which together, with their standardized forms and tables, make it easier for inspectors to manage campus assets. For students, there is a study schedule app that provides academic information, including the course name, lecturer bio, place, and time; the academic calendar; a list of important dates for students and staff; and even a route map for how to get to specific classes or labs. Additionally, there is a geonotifications app that administrators can use to send alerts to university staff, faculty, students, and visitors about specific events or emergencies. Users will receive these notifications on their cell phones based on their location or nearby events.

To get the mobile portal and its apps working well, the Openware team developed a web app to manage the administration web page. Users with administrative permissions can set roles and privileges for other users and administer and configure push notifications.

Because the flow of data through SSUC-KU's GIS, typically called flow of transmittals, is so massive, the Openware team needed a dynamic dashboard to control the process. Built with ArcGIS Dashboards, it shows the number of transmittals by month, discipline, project, and business. It also shows the review results for submitted packets of data, which are designated as approved, rejected, or accepted with notes. To show these statistics on the dashboard, it was necessary to design an ArcSDE table that specific users can access and edit to keep information up-to-date. Editing and tracking are also enabled so that management can know who is doing what and when.

At the campus level, water and electricity networks are managed and updated using Esri partner Schneider Electric's ArcFM™ solution, which is installed on top of ArcGIS Desktop. The campus's telecommunications network, however, is managed and updated using GDi Ensemble from Esri's official distributor in Croatia, GDi.

Planning the next campus

With SSUC-KU's health sciences campus currently under design, the project team is incorporating even more sophisticated enterprise technology. To support the operations and decision-making processes, for example, this campus's building data will be delivered in a building information modeling (BIM) format that is compatible with the university's current GIS schema. This will allow staff at SSUC-KU to simulate all the buildings and their complete services, including water, electricity, and telecommunications. When the health campus is fully designed and construction begins, the flow of transmittals in both GIS and BIM formats will be incorporated into SSUC-KU's geodatabase, further enriching the campus's GIS content.

A version of this story originally appeared as "New Kuwait University Campus Incorporates GIS from the Outset" in the Summer 2019 issue of *ArcNews*.

GIS IMPROVES ESTATE MANAGEMENT

University of Cambridge

THE ESTATE MANAGEMENT TEAM FOR THE UNIVERSITY OF Cambridge in Cambridge, England, has a substantial operational estate to maintain. Besides planning for and managing the organization's estate development program, it is also charged with promoting the university's environmental sustainability initiative. In 2018, the Space Data team created a digital Estate Map in ArcGIS Online, converting data from multiple file formats, and introduced new processes to provide accurate estate information to staff and stakeholders.

The challenge

With more than 350 operational buildings to sustain and keep secure and safe and nearly 700 acres of land to maintain, the University of Cambridge's Estates Division manages an operational estate currently valued at £3 billion (insurance replacement cost, February 2019). The complex nature of the estate presents many challenges, from looking after the University Farm and buildings over 800 years old, Grade I listed and protected by English Heritage, to highly specialized buildings used for teaching and research. In addition, there is an investment portfolio of leased residential and commercial properties. As a collegiate university, Cambridge comprises a University Estate that includes college properties outside of Cambridge. But they were not included in the map of the University Estate proper.

The Estates Division's Space Data team is responsible for maintaining source data and keeping an up-to-date record of all CAD drawings and floor plans of the university's buildings. A major frustration for the team was not being able to show this data on a single map in a more detailed way. The university's official map was limited, showing Cambridge only, whereas the estate has buildings and land assets outside of Cambridge, in Ely, Leicester, and London. The team also relied on a supply of data updates and new additions from colleagues across the department.

The Space Data team was looking for a way to improve processes and facilitate improved sharing of information across the university, with people of different skill levels. Although the team had no previous working knowledge of GIS, it was keen to identify a system that could maintain data and provide accurate estate information to staff and stakeholders.

The solution

Following its attendance at an Association of University Directors of Estates (AUDE) facilities management event, the Space Data team recognized the potential of ArcGIS as the software platform that could not only fulfill its primary requirements but also create a valuable gateway to further information and functions. The university had been using ArcGIS as a teaching tool for years, but the technology had not previously been used for the administration of data and asset management or as a sharing and collaboration tool.

"We were really keen to learn how we could use ArcGIS to improve processes and to make our work more visible, making it easier for people to understand what we own and what we have an interest in," said Dawn Birch, estate data coordinator for the Space Data team.

Initially, the team used ArcGIS Pro to convert its CAD data to GIS formats to use in ArcGIS Online. Processes were put in place to manage all internal data and make it accessible in an organized folder structure. When the data was visualized in a digital Estate Map, it was the first time that the entirety of the estate's holdings could be seen and explored in one place. Using existing CAD data appended to OS MasterMap data, extruded by building height, the new 3D map delivered a completely different perspective of the whole campus.

In terms of data collection, estate surveys had previously used unreliable paper-based collection. The Space Data team replaced this process with mobile data collection using the Survey123 app, a digital solution that works on smart devices, laptops, or desktops, even in disconnected environments. Surveyors were able to highlight more precise details of where buildings and assets, such as bicycle sheds, are located and, having purchased a new global navigation satellite system (GNSS) receiver, are now working alongside their IT colleagues on hosting and updating the entire cable network within ArcGIS.

The Space Data team also joined Esri's Early Adopter Community, giving them the opportunity to try the latest Esri technology before its public release.

Benefits

Consolidating the estate holdings into one map led to the following benefits:

Improved sharing of information

Estate holdings are more transparent and visible through the digital Estate Map and can be viewed and explored in one place. The map replaces previous silos of data and information held across different departments, making vital information and accurate updates and additions available to stakeholders across the organization. The ArcGIS Explorer mobile app also gives colleagues access to data and the digital Estate Map while out and around the estate.

Better use of existing data

The team can now view and map biodiversity data related to the estate, visualizing existing data that they had previously been unable to visualize and share. This data includes where current land is in relation to buildings, site boundaries, city wildlife sightings, local nature reserves, and water features.

Process improvements and increased operational efficiency

Digital re-creation of previously paper-based surveys has resulted in significant resource savings. Office-based employees no longer need to manually enter data on spreadsheets and in databases because it can be undertaken in real time by surveyors on the estate, using ArcGIS mobile apps.

Supporting future planning

Multiple projects using ArcGIS have been earmarked to support better decision-making regarding both asset management and sustainability goals. These include tree surveys, sustainability maps, and accommodation plans. Because the university already used ArcGIS for teaching purposes, it has been able to extend its use of ArcGIS for minimal cost.

A version of this story originally appeared as "University of Cambridge: Enhanced Data Collection and Management Delivering Improved Processes and Sharing of Information" on esriuk.com in July 2019.

IT'S IN THE WASTEWATER: SENSING AND MAPPING COVID-19

University of California San Diego

BY MIDSUMMER 2021, THE DELTA VARIANT HAD BECOME widespread, toppling any optimism that the COVID-19 pandemic might end soon. But a team at the University of California San Diego (UCSD) had already spotted this new threat. There it was, the virus's RNA sequence, in campus wastewater samples.

Rather than cause alarm, the presence of the more infectious COVID-19 variant offered the team hope. Here was evidence that its epidemiological strategy could detect the Delta variant and, likely, any future mutations.

The UCSD program to detect and communicate COVID-19 cases involved daily wastewater testing. Results were tied to a live map, created with GIS, to show which university buildings had a positive reading. The virus sensing effort from sewage led to early viral testing recommendations for individuals, which, in turn, helped curb campus spread. This effort enabled UCSD to offer on-campus housing and in-person classes and research opportunities through most of the pandemic.

Although other campuses have attempted similar screening programs, few reached UCSD's scale or efficiency. To be successful, the system had to provide near real-time information. As evidence of its achievement, the UCSD team was tapped to monitor wastewater for the city of San Diego's 1.4 million residents using the same process.

How UCSD led its Return to Learn

The campus setting proved to be an ideal location for devising disease surveillance systems and curbing the spread of COVID-19, even though people were living and working in close quarters.

The university launched its Return to Learn program with three pillars: risk mitigation, viral detection, and intervention. The university's Office of Operational Strategic Initiatives led the effort, with Rob Knight, professor and director of the Center for Microbiome Innovation, as the chief laboratory investigator.

Concerned that outbreaks could occur and spread rapidly in buildings with high occupancy, Knight and his team began testing wastewater to safely maintain the campus population during the pandemic and take early action when needed.

Often, infected students were not aware they had the virus. In the summer of 2020, the system detected a positive case one Friday afternoon. Notifications went out within 14 hours, and that weekend more than 650 people were tested.

The Return to Learn team credited transparency as the key to participation. Detailed maps of every building, pipe, and sewage access point formed the basemap. A public GIS dashboard showed

The Return to Learn collaboration at UCSD expanded to academic researchers, students, and campus staff, including facilities management, planning, emergency response, health, dining and hospitality, and other departments.

daily updates of monitored buildings, sampled water, and detected virus. The dashboard kept the entire campus community abreast of the university's viral infection status.

"It's not just our processing of the data but being able to share that data out to everyone and the public," said Natasha Martin, an associate professor in the Department of Medicine, Division of Infectious Diseases and Global Public Health, at UCSD. "We have people that visit, and they can check on the public dashboard and see if a particular building was positive on that day."

Despite early uncertainty about how well the system would detect cases, it proved to be extremely sensitive, Martin said. More than 85 percent of the university's residential cases were detected in the wastewater.

Showing students and staff where the virus is

At the outset, UCSD had just six wastewater autosamplers that captured effluent for laboratory testing. The results were recorded manually on a spreadsheet. But soon the university was sampling the wastewater in 350 buildings every day, and the results were automatically added to the map.

To achieve automation, UCSD created a better map that included sewer system pathways to correlate wastewater samples collected in pipes to the buildings they served. Once a building was identified, the university traced the virus to individuals through standard nasal-swab testing.

During the summer of 2020, the Return to Learn team began issuing notifications to campus residents and staff by email, lobby flyers, and even door-to-door knocking to compel further testing. To the surprise of Martin and others, it worked. When people received notifications of positive wastewater samples, individual testing rates increased as much as thirteenfold. The testing prompted a quick start to isolation and contact tracing.

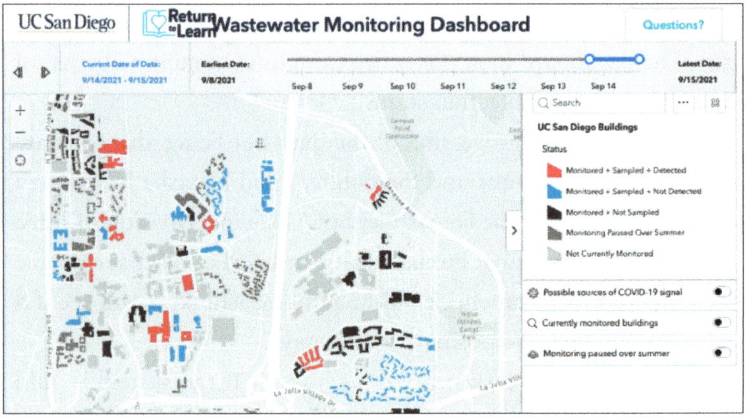

The GIS trace tool automatically pushes wastewater test results to a public map and notification repository. A suite of Esri tools, including ArcGIS Pro, ArcGIS Online, ArcGIS Notebooks, ArcGIS Dashboards, and ArcGIS Survey123, was used for different elements of the wastewater monitoring effort.

Automation involves robots, dashboards, maps, and mass emails

To alert people on campus of a positive result, the team couldn't rely on a time-consuming multistep lab process. Backlogs and delays would derail the promise of wastewater testing. To speed the process, UCSD introduced robots to the lab and automated the notification systems.

A group of students and staff gathered every morning to collect sewage samples across the campus, using liquid-handling collection robots, and then returned to the lab for processing. There, robots concentrated the virus using magnetic nanoparticles and then extracted RNA—genetic material that makes up the genomes of viruses such as SARS-CoV-2—from the samples. Polymerase chain reaction testing was then used to search for the virus's signature genes.

The automated, high-throughput system could process 24 samples every 40 minutes. Data was then added to a digital dashboard and map that tracked new positive cases building by building.

If Martin already knew that a student was isolating in a building from which a positive sample returned, she didn't issue a notification. The notification process was otherwise fully automated. Martin provided the dates of positivity and the sampler number, and emails were sent automatically to everyone living or working in that building.

She estimated that automation initially saved her two to three hours of work per day. Without automation, it would have been hard to expand the scale of the wastewater testing effort

Expanding beyond the campus

With the promise of curtailing future epidemics and pandemics, wastewater surveillance could be a university's or community's greatest early warning system. Recognizing the efficacy of wastewater testing, the US Centers for Disease Control and Prevention launched its National Wastewater Surveillance System in September 2020.

"We hope wastewater-based epidemiology will become more widely adopted," Knight said in March 2021. "Rapid, large-scale infectious disease early alert systems could be particularly useful for community surveillance in vulnerable populations and communities with less access to diagnostic testing and fewer opportunities to distance and isolate—during this pandemic, and the next."

A version of this story by Este Geraghty originally appeared as "It's in the Wastewater: How UC San Diego Senses and Maps COVID-19" on the *Esri Blog* on September 28, 2021.

CROWDSOURCING A UNIVERSITY'S FACILITIES MAPPING

Washington State University

AFTER 40 YEARS OF RAPID EXPANSION OF ITS MORE THAN 1,700-acre campus, Washington State University (WSU) found that its utility maps—which were primarily paper based—had become inaccessible and inaccurate. Using ArcGIS technologies and Microsoft Silverlight development tools, the university created a crowdsourcing web app that enabled every member of the 375-person facilities department to view the same maps and data. More importantly, this data can be updated as facilities staff members work on-site.

Growing pains

Founded in 1890, WSU has experienced several large construction booms during its long history. Major renovations to numerous facilities on the main campus in Pullman, Washington, caused massive changes to the utility systems. The university's utility maps became out-of-date and led to many surprises for crews working on-site. To get by, crews resorted to creating and redlining their own paper maps. (Redlining refers to corrections made on-site.)

In 2011, WSU Facilities Services was formed by bringing the Facilities Operations and Capital Projects departments together. New leadership and new department priorities opened the doors to further development of the department's existing GIS. At the time, GIS had been used for tracking university-owned real estate. Although utility data was populated in the GIS, it had not been incorporated into the departmental workflow.

Users can overlay current GIS data on construction civil drawings to see what changes will be made to utilities over the course of a building project.

Developing a solution

The goal was simple: create an easy-to-use mobile app so that all staff could view and query the same geospatial data as well as contribute information to the university's GIS.

Creating a user interface that would provide a rich and inviting user experience was a top priority. Getting people who were more comfortable with paper maps to use the mobile app was already a challenging proposition. Facilities Services wanted staff not only to use the app but also use it for correcting data.

At the time, Facilities Services was using Microsoft Silverlight and the Expression Blend integration development environment (IDE), so creating an engaging user experience was relatively easy.

Embracing the use of touch screens for the app was important so users could edit utility data on-site on a tablet. Menu items had to be easy to select and interact with while holding the tablet, so the menu structure allowed users to use their thumbs to choose menu items. This not only made the app easy to use but allowed the maximum amount of screen real estate for the map.

The menus were designed as a stack of cards located offscreen. To transition between menus, clean, fluid animations "fly" the card in and out of view as needed. Using this method created infinite scalability because the app isn't limited to a finite menu content area. If menu content is needed, a new card is flown in. It is flown out when the user is done with it. App functionality can be continually added without constant reworking of the entire user interface—another bonus.

Creating familiarity

Good design only goes so far when enticing people to use an app. This is especially true when users' accustomed workflow must be replaced with a new one. In this case, users had kept their own paper

By allowing crews to redline utility information on-site, UCSD can quickly update decades of missed changes to utility system maps.

utility maps with handwritten markups (redlines) for years. Showing them an app containing different map data wasn't going to work.

So, the paper maps that users had been working with were scanned and georeferenced by an intern so they could be converted to a mosaic dataset. After this mosaic dataset was published as an image service, users could view their old maps in the new app. This created instant familiarity. The bonus was that it allowed everyone in the department to see all the maps for the first time. Previously, these maps were available to only a small group in the organization.

Starting to correct bad data

Policy changes on how as-built drawings were handled and incorporated into records after a project's completion were a necessary first step in correcting current and future WSU utility data. However, this process didn't address the many decades of sporadic and missed updates to the campus's utility maps.

The GIS team consists of just two full-time employees and several student interns, so there was no way they could update errors in old records while keeping up with new construction projects. The team turned to crowdsourced cartography. Facilities Services staff members knew the utility systems better than anyone and could update the maps while they worked on-site. Data could be fixed efficiently and accurately while providing everyone in the organization with immediate access to the corrections.

When a utilities crew member finds a feature in the field that isn't in the GIS, that feature can be added by opening the Redlines menu in the app, selecting the appropriate utility system, selecting the component to add or remove, and placing the feature on the map. The user can also add attributes to the new feature.

Redlines are saved to their own feature class in ArcSDE® and appear on the map as red symbols. This symbology indicates that a redline feature has not had its exact location verified or committed to the permanent record.

The CAD manager, using a specially designed GIS dashboard, can see when a redline feature has been recorded. The manager then investigates the addition or deletion to determine whether it exists in an old as-built drawing that was never incorporated into the GIS. If no record is found, a student intern goes out to capture its exact location, using a GPS unit with centimeter accuracy. Next, using AutoCAD Map 3D, the manager transfers the redline feature into the proper ArcSDE feature class.

It's an efficient and effective process. Using this method, 118 features in one system were located and corrected in just four days. What's more, crews can now make a difference for the whole organization.

Filling data voids

Crowdsourced cartography proved successful in correcting project-related changes from the past. However, another issue remained: the amount of time it took to receive as-built drawings after the completion of a major construction project. Depending on the complexity of a project, it could take years to receive the as-built drawings. This delay could lead to situations in which Facilities Services performed remodeling to a facility before receiving the original as-built drawing.

Filling this data void required coming up with a different way of showing project-related changes to the utilities systems for a site. The latest construction set of civil drawings was turned into an image service by scanning the drawings and displaying them in the app. This allows users to overlay GIS data onto the civil drawings and see what changes have been made to utilities for that site. Because the app shows the complete civil drawing, the user can see that it was part of the construction set and not an official as-built drawing.

Results

The app took a year to develop, and by 2015, there were more than 175 active users of the GIS. GIS is now accessed by all four main campuses at WSU and is used as a planning and discussion tool during meetings. Because of its inviting and intuitive user experience and additional features such as access to old paper maps, the app was successful in meeting the goal of being widely adopted within the organization.

A version of this story by Bob Nichols originally appeared as "Crowdsourcing a University's Facilities Mapping" in the Winter 2015 issue of *ArcUser*.

NEXT STEPS

The Geographic Approach to education

EVERYONE IN EDUCATION, FROM STUDENTS TO FACULTY TO campus facility managers, can benefit from the spatial thinking fostered by the application of GIS and The Geographic Approach. Our world is rapidly changing. At the same time, GIS is rapidly evolving, while societal expectations continue to change. These resources can help you keep learning and growing in your ongoing geospatial journey.

For links to these and other GIS resources, visit the companion web page for this book at go.esri.com/casc-resources.

Educator resources

Resources include free, standards-based, textbook-aligned activities, instructional materials, and content that teachers can master in minutes. These are available on the web for a variety of subjects to enhance inquiry-based learning for students. Materials for ArcGIS Online require no installations or logins and work well on any connected computer, laptop, or tablet.

- **GeoInquiries:** GeoInquiries™ are short, standards-based inquiry activities for teaching map-based content found in commonly used textbooks. Each activity is designed using a common inquiry model and can be presented quickly from a single computer and projector or modified for students' hands-on engagement. Collections of 15–20 activities per topic enhance your curriculum throughout the year.

- **"Mapping Our World":** World geography classroom instructional materials that use ArcGIS Online. The materials and web maps are curated by the Esri Education Team. Another version of these materials is available for ArcGIS Desktop 10.
- **"Thinking Spatially Using GIS":** This resource offers free elementary geography instructional materials for ArcGIS Online. No login or additional software is required. "Thinking Spatially Using GIS" was developed to enhance spatial learning for upper elementary students and to provide teachers with comprehensive and easy-to-use resources for GIS instruction in the classroom. Updated teacher and student materials are available at no cost to download and use in classroom instruction.
- **Career and technical education:** Learn about GIS careers for students and ArcGIS classroom instruction for career and technical education (CTE) teachers.
- **The ArcGIS Books:** Explore big ideas in mapping in this book series. The ArcGIS Books are your interactive, learn-by-doing guides to using GIS for better decision-making.
- **Teach with GIS:** The new Teach with GIS hub experience is for educators looking for interesting labs that feature real-world, scenario-driven exercises designed for classroom instruction. Get access to hands-on learning materials that can be used to encourage science, technology, engineering, arts, and mathematics (STEAM) education and explore topics in geography, the social sciences, and history. The content is designed for K–12 students.

- **Learn ArcGIS:** This instructional website hosts scenario-based, hands-on lessons with free access to ArcGIS Online, ArcGIS Pro, and other apps.
- **Free software for instruction:** The ArcGIS for Schools bundle is available to schools at no cost and includes apps for mobile devices, tablets, web browsers, and desktop computers.
- ***Spatial Reserves*:** This book and blog focus on where to find geospatial data, how to know whether that data is accurate, and societal issues such as ethics, copyright, and location privacy.

Researcher resources

Resources for researchers include open source geospatial projects, documentation, and key competencies.

- **Esri open source:** Explore more than 500 geospatial projects showing how people are thinking spatially and solving problems together.
- **ArcGIS documentation:** Discover everything you want to know about ArcGIS. Access tool references, code samples, tutorials, answers to frequently asked questions (FAQ), and more.
- **GIS&T Body of Knowledge:** Discover the foundations of geographic information science and associated technologies (GIS&T) through key essays written by leading GIS&T instructors.

- **Geospatial Technology Competency Model:** Examine the key competencies in geospatial technology and spatial thinking compiled by educators working closely with the US Department of Labor's Employment and Training Administration and GeoTech Center.

IT support resources

Resources for IT support include best practices; security, privacy, and compliance information; technical support; and technical training.

Best practices for managing ArcGIS

Staff at leading universities have developed recommendations for managing ArcGIS as an enterprise resource to maximize access and minimize administration time.

- Learn to manage ArcGIS usage.
- Build a dashboard to monitor usage.
- See more resources for administrators.

ArcGIS Trust Center

As education moves increasingly online, information security and privacy become increasingly important. ArcGIS Trust Center is your go-to resource for security, privacy, and compliance information.

- Go to the ArcGIS Trust Center.
- Read the Esri Privacy Statement.
- Explore ArcGIS Security Advisor.

Technical support services

Your institution's license includes help from Esri technical support services and a global community of users.

- Contact Esri Technical Support for help.
- Tap into Esri Community for help.
- Learn more about Esri Support Services.

Training and learning resources

Your institution's license includes access to technical training for both IT administrators and end users.

- Explore Esri Academy.
- Find guided lessons at Learn ArcGIS.
- Browse Esri Press books.

Administrator resources

Reources for administrators include tools for campus facilities, utilities, and health and safety.

Campus facilities

Integrate campus and building data to better understand the complex needs of the spaces you manage and maintain.

- **Learn ArcGIS:** Learn how to implement ArcGIS Indoors for COVID-19 facility mapping response, to see who and what is within walking or driving distance of your facility, and more.

- **ArcGIS Solutions:** The Road Closures solution can be used to maintain an inventory of road closures and communicate closures and detours to travelers. The Public Parking solution can be used to inventory parking assets (lots, garages, on-street spaces, and pay stations), and more.

Campus utilities

Provide information to everyone who needs it to keep your utilities running smoothly.

- **Learn ArcGIS:** Model, analyze, diagram, and work with your network data using ArcGIS Utility Network. Create attribute rules and pop-up expressions to enforce and report on data integrity within a utility network and more.
- **ArcGIS Solutions:** Use the Participatory Budgeting solution to solicit feedback and prioritize spending projects. Use the Capital Project Planning solution to define a project portfolio and share your plan with internal and external stakeholders, and more.

Campus health and safety

Prevent, protect against, and mitigate the effects of threats and hazards in your campus community.

- **Learn ArcGIS:** Visualize and analyze crime incidents to identify areas with higher auto thefts to help recommend theft reduction strategies, create risk maps for COVID-19 transmission, and more.
- **ArcGIS Solutions:** Use the Coronavirus Business Continuity solution to maintain business operations and share authoritative information with stakeholders. Use the Crime Analysis solution to enhance public safety and plan crime prevention strategies, and more.

Learn more

For links to these and other GIS resources, visit the companion web page for this book at:

go.esri.com/casc-resources

CONTRIBUTORS

Tom Baker
Matt Ball
Jim Baumann
Chris Chiappinelli
George Dailey
Charlie Fitzpatrick
Michael Gould
Angela Lee
Geri Miller
Tom Miller
Patty Mims
Monica Pratt
Adena Schutzberg
Citabria Stevens
Carla Wheeler

ABOUT ESRI PRESS

AT ESRI PRESS, OUR MISSION IS TO INFORM, INSPIRE, AND teach professionals, students, educators, and the public about GIS by developing print and digital publications. Our goal is to increase the adoption of ArcGIS and to support the vision and brand of Esri. We strive to be the leader in publishing great GIS books, and we are dedicated to improving the work and lives of our global community of users, authors, and colleagues.

Acquisitions

Stacy Krieg
Claudia Naber
Alycia Tornetta
Craig Carpenter
Jenefer Shute

Editorial

Carolyn Schatz
Mark Henry
David Oberman

Production

Monica McGregor
Victoria Roberts

Marketing

Sasha Gallardo
Beth Bauler

Contributors

Christian Harder
Matt Artz
Keith Mann

Business

Catherine Ortiz
Jon Carter
Jason Childs

For information on Esri Press books and resources, visit our website at esri.com/en-us/esri-press.